WISDOM EACH DAY

Rabbi Abraham J. Twerski, M.D.

Av – Elul
July – September

COMPLIMENTS
OF

Amram Kass, PC • 555 Madison Avenue • New York, NY 10022

❖ SPONSORS ❖

Worldwide Equipment Co.
Livonia, Michigan

✈

Madison Title Agency, LLC

✈

Prestige Caterers

✈

Sterling Insurance Concepts

✈

Eretz Funding, LTD

✈

Preferred Health Mate Inc.

SHALOM
TORAH
CENTERS
מוסדות שלום לחינוך ילדים

SHALOM TORAH CENTERS: EDUCATING GENERATIONS

Just across the Hudson River, close to the dynamic Jewish centers of New York City, lies the State of New Jersey. Except for a few enclaves of strong Jewish awareness, crossing this river is like crossing into another world. For the more than half a million Jews residing in cities and suburban towns across New Jersey, traditional Judaism may, unfortunately, become something of the past. Their children, conveniently blended into the local public school system, will never be given the opportunity to discover the singular beauty of our Torah, its heritage and traditions. At worst, these Jewish children will intermarry and be forever lost to our people. At best, they will carry their Jewishness through life as an unwelcome burden, and their own children will be that much further from the rest of us. We stand today – literally – facing the disappearance of thousands of families from our nation, unless we can reach out and pull them back from oblivion.

In a courageous effort, a group of Torah scholars from Beth Medrash Govoha in Lakewood, New Jersey, joined together in the early '70s to create the Shalom Torah Centers. Although committed to spreading the light of Torah to all the Jewish people of New Jersey, Shalom Torah Centers began with the children.

The first Shalom Torah Center, an afternoon Hebrew school, was established in Manalapan Township in 1973 with an enrollment of thirty-one children. Viewed from the perspective of the overall situation, it was a nick in a mountainous problem, but it was a beginning nonetheless. Viewed from an individual perspective, however, it represented thirty-one victories, for every Jewish child is priceless in its own right. Every Jewish child carries with it the prayers and sacrifices of countless generations of its forebears and the hope for all future generations.

Looking back, the first thirty years have been a time of growth and consolidation for Shalom Torah Centers. That first small school has grown into a blossoming network of Talmud Torahs and Hebrew Day Schools — that collectively reach hundreds of Jewish children — *shuls, mikvaos,* and a highly effective and comprehensive Adult Education program.

In Twin Rivers the Morris Namias Shalom Torah Academy is credited

Continued on back page

"The beneficiary of a miracle may not recognize the miracle" *(Niddah 31a).*

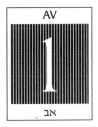

AV

אב

Rosh Chodesh

July 19, 2004
Aug. 6, 2005

From the Sages

Some people ask, "Why do we no longer see miracles like those in the Scriptures?" This question was posed to the Chofetz Chaim by the proprietor of an inn where he was lodging. The Chofetz Chaim said he would answer his question in a short while.

In the afternoon, the innkeeper's daughter returned from school. She proudly showed her parents a certificate she had received for excellence in memorizing and reciting poetry. The Chofetz Chaim asked the child to recite some poetry. The child, apparently shy, refused to do so. The Chofetz Chaim asked the innkeeper to tell his child to recite the poetry. The child refused and said, "I don't have to show everyone. Here is the certificate that tells that I can do it."

The Chofetz Chaim said to the innkeeper, "There was a time when G-d did miracles to show us that He is the Master and is in control of the world. We have the Torah as the certificate of His might and power. Like your daughter, He doesn't have to show His power to everyone. The certificate should suffice."

The fact is that miracles constantly occur. We say this in the *Amidah*, when we thank G-d for "the miracles that are daily with us." It is just that we do not recognize the miracles as such.

People sometimes think of some things as coincidences. It has been wisely said that "coincidences are nothing other than miracles in which G-d wished to remain anonymous."

A tiny seed is planted in the ground. It disintegrates, and before long a tiny sprout appears. Over the years it grows into a tree which produces abundant fruit year after year. The only reason we do not recognize this amazing occurrence as a miracle is because we are accustomed to it.

A wise person is not easily deceived. He recognizes the miracles which occur every day.

From Our Heritage

We have today unprecedented opportunities to study Torah.

The Midrash states that an unlearned person who sees Torah scholars may despair of being able to learn. "I can never become a scholar," he may say. "I hardly know the *aleph-beis.*"

The Midrash states that two hungry people entered into a room and saw a loaf of bread on a high shelf beyond their reach. One was a fool and said, "Forget it! There is no way we can reach that bread."

The other said, "That bread did not get up there by itself. The way someone was able to put it up there is the way we can get it down."

Torah scholars were not born erudite. At one time they hardly knew the *aleph-beis.* By continuous study they progressed to become great scholars. There is nothing that prevents anyone from doing likewise.

NOTES

From the Scriptures

"There is an evil which I have seen under the sun, like an error which proceeds from a ruler" *(Ecclesiastes 10:5)*.

The psalmist says, "Guard your tongue from evil and your lips from speaking deceit" *(Psalms 34:14)*. This is no easy task, and Solomon takes it one step further. He cautions us not to *inadvertently* say something inappropriate. Solomon compares a word spoken in error to a pronouncement of a ruler. When a king orders someone executed, his command is promptly obeyed. Though he may later realize that this was not the person he wanted executed, it is unfortunately too late. The person cannot be brought back to life. Similarly, a statement made in error may have irreversible consequences. Thoughtless words may result in unintended harm to others. It is no consolation that the harm was unintended.

Is it realistic to expect people to think before they speak? It certainly is. We hold a person responsible for damage he may do because of negligence in wielding a sharp knife. The prophet says, "The tongue is like a sharp arrow" *(Jeremiah 9:7)*. One is equally responsible for damage done because of negligence in speech.

This is one time that one may consider himself wise and important. The Talmud says that wise people should be careful as to what they say *(Ethics of the Fathers 1:11)*. Speaking in a way that can be misinterpreted can have serious consequences. No one should think, "I can say what I wish. No one takes my words as authoritative." Here one must think of himself as wise, and excercise caution regarding what he says lest his talk cause unintended harm.

This is another example of the Talmudic dictum, "Silence serves as a fence to protect wisdom" *(Ethics of the Fathers 3:17)*.

From Our Heritage

NOTES

In Radin there was a scholar who craved honor. He would engage the students in Talmudical discussions to demonstrate his erudition. He was aware that he was not highly regarded. On the other hand, he saw the enormous respect and honor accorded to the Chofetz Chaim. He was unable to restrain himself and asked the Chofetz Chaim, "We are both Torah scholars. Why is it that you command such respect, whereas I am the object of disdain?"

The Chofetz Chaim responded, "The Talmud states that if anyoneone pursues acclaim, it flees from him, but acclaim follows anyone who flees it *(Eruvin 13b)*. The secret is in the word 'anyone.' One who pursues acclaim, even a fine Torah scholar like you, will not get it. On the other hand, if one shuns acclaim, it will follow him even if he is as undeserving and unlearned as I am.

"You deserve to be honored because of your extensive knowledge, but you drive it away by your pursuing honor. I know I am not deserving of honor, and I am irritated when I am given honor that I do not merit. That is why it follows me."

"**E**ither friendship or death!" *(Taanis 23a).*

The Talmud relates that the sage Choni fell into a deep sleep for seventy years. When he awoke, he went into the *beis midrash.* When the students had difficulties in understanding something and he clarified it for them, they remarked, "Why, this person illuminates things like the sage Choni."

"I am Choni!" he said. Being that Choni had lived seventy years earlier, they did not believe him. Finding himself with no peers to whom he could relate, Choni exclaimed, "If I cannot have any friends, I would rather be dead!"

JJuly 21, 2004
Aug. 8, 2005

There are three relationships essential for a happy life: A teacher, a friend, and a student. We must have someone from whom to learn, someone whom to teach, and someone with whom to share.

In the family scheme, we learn from our parents, teach our children and share with a spouse. The Talmud says that a man who is without a wife is not a complete person (*Yevamos* 63a). Socially, we learn from teachers, teach students, and share with friends.

It appears that sharing is of greater importance than learning from teachers. Choni obviously had no teachers, but did not find that this made life intolerable. But he could not live without a friend.

We must be careful that we do not harbor traits that pose obstacles to friendship. Among these is envy; we cannot be comfortable with someone whom we envy. Another is low self-esteem. In *Life's Too Short* I point out that people who feel inferior and unworthy may withdraw from relationships.

Wise people will realize the importance of sharing, and will try to eliminate the traits that stand in the way of friendship.

From Our Heritage

The Chofetz Chaim was once traveling in a coach. The driver complained that his horse had died. The townspeople took up a collection to buy him another horse, and he was embarrassed to have taken charity. Why did he deserve this? Why did G-d do this to him?

The Chofetz Chaim told him that all G-d's ways are just. Perhaps he had not been completely honest in his money dealings. Had he never quoted passengers a price, only to raise it along the way, giving the passengers no choice but to pay?

The driver admitted having done this. "But you are a *tzaddik*," he said. "You are always honest. Why was your coat stolen at the inn?"

The Chofetz Chaim said, "You think I am a *tzaddik*? I also have taken people's money unjustly. I check each book I sell to ensure that the binding is intact and that there are no damaged pages. But I am not perfect. I probably overlooked a bad book, and the buyer is hesitant to bring it for exchange. I have cheated someone. Even inadvertent theft is theft. I was punished for not being more careful."

It is at times like this that G-d says to the heavenly angels, "Look at the creature I have created!"

July 22, 2004
Aug. 9, 2005

From the Scriptures | "**M**oses went amongst his brethren and saw in their suffering" *(Exodus 2:11).*

Rashi comments, "He set his eyes and heart to agonize with them." The Midrash adds that Moses put his shoulder under the heavy burdens which the Israelites carried. To feel their suffering, it was not enough to observe. He had to identify with them.

Identifying with others is essential in any helping relationship. In *Positive Parenting* I point out that parents should be able to identify with their children. *If you want another to do something, you must see things through their eyes.* Moses could not feel the agony of the Israelites and become their leader until he felt their suffering as they did. He intensified this sensation by sharing their burden.

However, in order to help someone, you must be able to detach. The *shammas* of the Tolna rebbe noted the rebbe's garments to be soaked with perspiration after he received the petitions from his *chassidim.* He expressed his surprise, since the rebbe had not been exerting himself.

"I did not exert myself, you say? When a *chassid* comes to me with his problems, I cannot help him unless I identify with him and feel what he feels. I must shed my garments and put on his garments. But then I am as powerless to help him as he is to help himself. So I detach from the situation by shedding his garments and putting on mine. All morning I have been taking off garments and putting on garments, and you say I have not been exerting myself?"

The Tolna rebbe's formula is essential if we wish to be of help to anyone. Over-identification and total detachment preclude being of real help. It requires wisdom to know how much to identify and how much to detach.

From Our Heritage

NOTES

R' Hirsh of Rimanov, who is known in Chassidic lore as R' Hirsh *Meshores* (the servant), is one of the most inspiring of the Chassidic masters. His total self-development is described in *Not Just Stories.*

When the young, orphaned Hirsh came to the court of the *tzaddik* R' Mendel of Rimanov, he considered it a privilege to bring in the firewood. Eventually, he prevailed on R' Mendel's *shammas* to allow him to make the fire. He would recite the *Tehillim* with great fervor as he brought in the wood and made the fire. He was providing warmth for the *tzaddik,* and he felt this was no less a service than making the fire on the Altar of the Temple in Jerusalem.

Many years later, when R' Hirsh was an acclaimed rebbe with many *chassidim,* he used to long for the days when he made the fire for R' Mendel. "I could say the *Tehillim* with such *kavannah* (concentration) that I felt the fire burning in my heart. No one paid any attention to me. I could feel the lowly person I was. Today, with all the acclaim I receive, I must constantly remind myself how lowly I am indeed."

"J**oshua the son of Nun was filled with the spirit of wisdom because Moses had laid his hands upon him, so the children of Israel obeyed him"** *(Deuteronomy 34:9).*

From the Scriptures

July 23, 2004
Aug. 10, 2005

What is meant by "spirit of wisdom?"

In *Numbers* (27:18) G-d tells Moses to appoint Joshua, "a man in whom there is spirit" as his successor. At this time it is not mentioned that Joshua had a spirit "of wisdom." G-d instructed Moses, "You shall place some of your majesty upon him, so that the entire assembly of Israel will obey him" (*ibid.* 27:20).

The basis of spirituality is humility. Moses' humility is the only one of his traits discussed in the Torah. "The man Moses was exceedingly humble, more than any person" (*ibid.* 12:3). This humility gave rise to all commendable traits. *Targum Yonasan* states that Joshua, too, was exceedingly humble (*ibid.* 13:16). Thus, this Joshua was "a man in whom there is spirit," i.e., humility.

But a leader must know when to set aside humility and be authoritarian. Initially, Moses had only humility (*Exodus* 3:11); once he was leader, he acted with authority (*ibid.* 16:1-35). Knowing when to be humble and when to exercise authority takes wisdom.

This was Moses's majesty, and he invested Joshua with this majesty. The "man in whom there is spirit" thus became one "filled with the *spirit of wisdom,* so the children of Israel obeyed him."

Any leader—a parent, teacher, or community leader—must use a "spirit of wisdom" to be humble and yet exert authority.

True wisdom is a craving to know more. There is a proverb, "If you know all the answers, you haven't asked all the questions."

From Our Heritage

The Rebbe of Gur told of a wealthy scholar who sought a husband for his daughter. He went to a major yeshivah and asked the dean for the most accomplished students. The dean showed him three students. The scholar presented them with a vexing Talmudic problem, saying that whoever resolves the matter wins his daughter's hand.

Each of the students posed possible solutions, but the scholar rebutted all of them. When they failed to give a satisfactory answer, the scholar left, saying he would try another yeshivah.

As he left, one of the students followed him, asking for the correct explanation that would resolve the problem. The scholar said, "The answer will not do you any good. You did not succeed in winning my daughter."

The student said, "True. Since I could not give the answer, I do not deserve her. But I still wish to know the resolution of the problem."

The scholar was impressed. "You are the one I want for my daughter. Your desire to know is more important than knowing."

NOTES

From the Scriptures

"The wise in heart shall take mitzvos" *(Proverbs 10:8).*

The Talmud applies this verse to Moses who, as other Israelites borrowed gold and silver from the Egyptians, sought to fulfill Joseph's wish that his remains be taken to the Promised Land. While this shows piety and dedication, how does it show Moses' wisdom?

The Midrash states that the Israelites were aware of their ancestors' promise to Joseph, but they said that Joseph's honor dictated that only "the greatest" deal with his remains. Moses had a dilemma. He wanted to fulfill the promise, yet to take the job would mean he felt himself "the greatest," conlicting with his humility.

So Moses waited until all the Israelites were engaged in collecting valuables from the Egyptians. He used this opportunity to take Joseph's remains. He could then explain that he took the remains by default, because everyone else was otherwise occupied.

This is an important lesson. The Talmud says, "In a place where there is no man (i.e., a leader), strive to be a man" (*Ethics of the Fathers* 2:6). One must sometimes rise to an occasion because no one else is acting responsibly. While this may run counter to the person's humility, he may have no choice. But one should do so in a way that shows he considers himself no greater than others.

The ability to exert leadership yet not lose one's humility requires exercise of wisdom. The wise person will seek to do both.

From Our Heritage

The Baal Shem Tov prayed that it be revealed to him who will be next to him in *Gan Eden* (Paradise). It was revealed to him that it would be Yaakov ben Yosef, who lived in a distant village.

The Baal Shem went to the village and asked about the *tzaddik* Yaakov ben Yosef, but no one knew of him. At long last they told him there was a Yaakov ben Yosef, but he was no *tzaddik*. He was a rather uncouth woodcutter living in the outskirts of the village.

Upon meeting Yaakov, the Baal Shem was certain he was a *tzaddik* concealing his true identity. But after spending several days with him, the Baal Shem Tov realized that Yaakov was indeed a crude, ignorant person. And oddly, Yaakov ate copious amounts of food. The Baal Shem asked him about this, and Yaakov said:

"My father was in a group attacked by highway bandits. After taking the people's belongings, the bandits chose to make sport of the Jews, and threatened to kill them unless they kissed the crucifix. My father was very strong. He broke off a thick branch and attacked the robbers. He risked his life but would not kiss the crucifix.

"I saw that I must be very strong so if I am ever challenged to kiss a crucifix, I will be able to defend myself like my father. I eat to be strong. When I cut down trees, the chopping action makes my muscles strong. No one will ever be able to make me sin against G-d!"

The Baal Shem Tov understood. Every bite of food Yaakov took and every move he made with the axe was for *kiddush Hashem* (sanctifying the Name of G-d).

NOTES

AV

7

אב

July 25, 2004
Aug. 12, 2005

"**E**very *mitzvah* of the Torah declares, 'Be wise!' Every prohibition of the Torah declares, 'Do not be a fool!'" *(R' Bunim of Pschis'che).*

From the Sages

The Torah is unlike any other body of law. Not only is it Divine, the Midrash says that it is the "blueprint" according to which G-d designed the world (*Yalkut Shimoni Mishlei* 942). In other words, the Torah's laws are laws of nature, much as the "law" of gravity.

People can adapt within natural law, but they cannot change it. Airplanes can fly and satellites can be propelled into space, but they must conform to the laws of gravity. Similarly, we can adapt within the framework of Torah, but no law of Torah can be abrogated.

Moses said, "I have placed life and death before you … you shall choose life, so you will live" (*Deuteronomy* 30:19). Accepting Torah precepts is more than complying with G-d's will. It is recognizing and adapting to reality. Trying to defy reality has consequences.

The *mussar* authorities said that modern technology helps us understand the teachings of *mussar.* The telephone and recorders make us realize that every word we say can be heard and recorded at a great distance, i.e., in the records of the Heavenly Tribunal. Today we know that we will suffer the consequences of polluting the air and water if we gratify our industrial aspirations. We endanger human survival by tampering with the ozone layer. Some people ignore these dire warnings, which is nothing but foolhardy. Similarly, we should realize that we cannot tamper with Torah without negatively affecting the world.

R' Bunim merely restated the words of Moses. Wise people will heed them.

From Our Heritage

When R' Chaim Berlin was rabbi of Moscow, a man asked to speak to him in private. "My wife had a boy, and I would like the rabbi to do the *bris.*"

"Gladly," R' Chaim said. "But why the secrecy?"

"I make my living by selling appurtenances for the church and religious items for people. No one should discover that I am Jewish," the man said.

R' Chaim told the man to send away the household help. The *bris* was done secretly, without a *minyan.*

R' Chaim asked the man, "What motivated you to make a *bris*?"

The man responded, "I have drifted away from Judaism. I don't know whether circumstances will ever allow me to return. But what if my child discovers his origin and decides to live like a Jew should? How can I deny him this right?"

Some people are irresponsible and make irreversible decisions that deny their children the freedom to ever choose a Torah lifestyle. Is not their claim to be "liberal" the ulitmate hypocracy?

NOTES

From the Scriptures

"**E**ven a fool, when he keeps silent, may be thought wise" (Proverbs 17:28).

Very few things receive as much attention in ethics as speech, and rightly so. The Torah describes the creation of man as "G-d breathed into his nostrils a soul of life, and man became a living being" (Genesis 2:7). Onkeles translates "man became a speaking soul". The defining feature of a human being is the ability to speak. It is only proper that this unique ability be given the utmost consideration.

The Chofetz Chaim dedicated his life to curbing lashon hara (gossip). The ethical works are replete with discouraging lying and deceitful talk. Solomon adds another dimension.

Even the wisest people sometimes commit folly. They may be unaware of this, but others will detect this. The less we talk, the less are the chances that others will discover our folly. If curtailing speech were advised only for those who know they are not wise, the world would be full of prattle. "A lazy man is wiser in his own eyes than seven sensible counselors" (Proverbs 26:16). Since everyone is at risk of thinking themselves much wiser than they are, our salvation may lie in silence.

One of the Chassidic masters commented, "But then silence is deceptive. By keeping silent you may lead others to think you are wise. How can Solomon sanction deception?"

He answered, "The only other option is for the person to talk. But when a fool talks, it is because he thinks what he is saying is wise. Of the two options, it is preferable to be silent even if this deceives others rather than to talk and deceive yourself."

Wise people watch their words carefully.

From Our Heritage

NOTES

When an epidemic of cholera broke out in Vilna, people prayed for Divine mercy and many did teshuvah, hoping that this would bring merit to the community. Some people, instead of finding defects in themselves to correct, sought to incriminate others.

One man came to R' Yisrael of Salant, stating that he knew of some people who were not observing Yiddishkeit properly and were not doing teshuvah in this time of distress. R' Yisrael interrupted him before he could identify these people.

R' Yisrael said, "The Talmud says that the affliction of tzaraas is brought about by lashon hara (gossip). The Torah requires that the afflicted person be quarantined beyond the community limits. Why? Because when he is totally isolated from other people, he will not have the opportunity to look for their shortcomings. He will only have himself to think about, and in this way he may discover his own defects.

"Is it not preferable that you look for what you may correct within yourself rather than looking for faults in others?"

"I arose to open the door for my beloved... but my beloved had slipped by and was gone" *(Song of Songs 5:5-6).*

Fast of Tishah B'Av

[When 9 Av falls on the Sabbath the fast is observed on Sunday.]

July 27, 2004
Aug. 14, 2005

Opportunity often knocks, but it may also steal quietly away. We must be alert to take advantage of an opportunity when it arises.

Procrastinating can mean missing valuable opportunities. When Eliezer chose Rebecca as a wife for Isaac, her family asked that she stay home for a while. The Torah gives Eliezer's response as a lesson for all time. "Do not cause me to delay, inasmuch as G-d has made my mission successful" *(Genesis* 24:56). If what you are going to do is right, it is the will of G-d, so do it promptly. If what you are doing cannot be considered to be the will of G-d, why are you doing it?

The Midrash states that the word "now" is indicative of *teshuvah.* Once a person has discovered he did wrong, the time to correct it is *now.* Delay may result in failure to correct the wrong.

The yetzer hara knows that if a person is motivated to do something, that motivation may override the *yetzer hara's* objection. So he tells the person, "Of course you will do it, but not just now." In the interim, the person's motivation cools or other distractions arise.

There is a classic text on alcoholism titled *I'll Quit Tomorrow.* This is equally true of anything a person would rather not do.

Notice that the *yetzer hara* never suggests delaying gratifying temptation. To the contrary, it urges us to satisfy desires promptly.

A wise person simply reverses the strategy of the *yetzer hara:* Do what is right promptly, and delay gratification of desires.

From Our Heritage

When we pray for the ultimate Redemption, are we sincere?

R' Nachum of Chernobel lodged at an inn. Each midnight he recited prayers lamentating our exile, and his weeping awoke the innkeeper. "Is the rabbi sick?" the innkeeper asked.

R' Nachum explained that he was mourning the destruction of the Temple and the Jews being driven into exile. This was news to the innkeeper. R' Nachum explained, "We must pray to G-d for Moshiach and the Redemption. We will then all be united in the Holy Land."

The innkeeper said, "I must ask my wife about this." A few moments later he returned, saying, "My wife says we cannot leave the inn with our cows, goats, and chickens to go to the Holy Land."

R' Nachum tried to impress the innkeeper with the bitterness of being in exile. "We are constantly being attacked by bands of Tartars who plunder and kill us. Don't you understand why we need Moshiach to redeem us from exile?"

The innkeeper thought a bit, then his eyes lit up. "Let Moshiach come and take the Tartars to the Holy Land. We will stay here with our inn and with our cows, goats, and chickens."

Do we pray like R' Nachum or like the innkeeper?

NOTES

AV

אב

July 28, 2004
Aug. 15, 2005

From the Scriptures

"A person's spirit sustains him in sickness, but if the spirit is broken, who shall uplift it?"** *(Proverbs 18:14).*

The foresight of Torah is incredible. Only recently have we begun to understand the mind-body-spirit relationship. Solomon stated it clearly three thousand years ago!

What is a new discovery is the mechanism whereby emotions affect the bodily function in both health and disease. Anecdotal reports about the salutary effects of cheer on recovery and the detrimental effects of dejection abound. Norman Cousins' classic book, *Anatomy of an Illness,* testifies to recovery from serious illness via an upbeat attitude. There are scientifically validated reports of prolongation of life and improvement in quality of life of cancer patients who participated in support groups that elevated their mood. More recently, the method whereby emotions affect the body has been elucidated by Dr. Candice Pert in *Molecules of Emotion.*

Many centuries ago, our sages incorporated this principle in the prayer for the sick. We pray that G-d grant them *refuas hanefesh urefuas haguf,* healing of the spirit and healing of the body. Giving priority to healing of the spirit indicates its primacy in recovery.

This is why Torah gives such great importance to the *mitzvah* of *bikur cholim,* visiting the sick. Letting the sick person know that others care about him, and especially if one can say something to lift his spirits, promotes recovery. "One who visits the sick person decreases his illness by one sixtieth."

It is wise to promote one's own health and recovery by elevating one's mood, and to visit the sick in a way that elevates their spirits.

From Our Heritage

NOTES

_____
_____
_____
_____
_____
_____
_____
_____
_____

Our culture has made a grave mistake by permitting dissemination of blatant immorality via the media under protection of the First Amendment. Shouting "Fire!" in a crowded theater is not protected by freedom of speech. Neither should portrayal of violence and obscenity be tolerated under the guise of free speech. The idea that we can protect our children from these noxious influences is fallacious. These toxic influences should be eliminated.

The Rebbe of Talna said, "Years ago, when people wore sandals, they avoided puddles. When they began wearing closed shoes, they would walk through puddles. Now that there are galoshes and boots, they may walk into deep mud. It seems that they are unaware that they may be dragging the dirt into their homes."

People delude themselves that grading programs or inserting "v chips" can shield our children from violent and immoral influences. We seem to forget that mature people are also vulnerable to corruption.

If you do not wish to bring mud into your house, avoid it!

"Correct yourself first, then you may correct others" *(Bava Metzia 107b).* | *From the Sages*

We have alluded to the fact that we are creatures of habit and that we are reluctant to change. However, we frequently ask others to change, as if it were a simple task. A good guideline is this: *Before you ask another person to change, make some change in yourself.* This will invariably result in your being more patient with others.

This is really a simple thing to do. You do not have to make any radical change in yourself. Before you ask of someone else to make a change, hold your cup of coffee in your left hand if you regularly hold it in your right. Do this for two days. If you normally wear your wrist watch on your left wrist, put it on your right wrist for two days. By habit, you will look at your left wrist for the time, even though you really know that the watch is on your right wrist. These little changes will make you aware of how uncomfortable change may be, and you will be more tolerant of other people.

Too often we ask of others more than we demand of ourselves.

In *It's Not as Tough as You Think* I related an anecdote about Mahatma Ghandi, who was asked by parents to tell their child to abstain from sweets. Ghandi told them to return in two weeks. When they returned, Ghandi explained to the child that it was important for his health and growth that he avoid sweets.

The parents asked Ghandi why he did not tell the child this two weeks earlier. "Because," he said, "then I was eating sweets myself."

A wise person expects no more from others than from himself.

From Our Heritage

When the Austrian emperor granted civil rights to the Jews, there was widespread rejoicing. The students of R' Moshe Schreiber (author of *Chasam Sofer*) saw him in tears. "Why are you crying when the news is so good?" they asked.

R' Moshe replied, "A king had a minister of whom he was very fond. One time the minister joined a rebel group. He was arrested and sentenced to death. Because of their previous relationship, the king commuted his sentence to imprisonment, and promised that he would eventually pardon him.

"The minister was thrown into a dungeon where he suffered from deplorable conditions. He lived with the hope of a pardon. One day he was told that several people had been sent to him by the king. His spirits soared, as he hoped they were bringing his pardon. But when they came to him they said, 'The king has sent you new clothes, a fine mattress, and has instructed the jailer to give you better food.' The minister broke down crying. 'Why are you crying?' the men asked. 'Aren't you happy that the king is making your life here much more comfortable?'"

R' Moshe continued, "I was hoping for a release from Exile by Moshiach, but when all we get is a more comfortable exile, that means that G-d is not ready to redeem us yet."

AV

12

אב

July 30, 2004
Aug. 17, 2005

From
the
Scriptures

"**There** is a friend who is more closely attached than a brother" *(Proverbs 18:24).*

"**On** the day of your misfortune do not come to your relative's house; better is a near neighbor than a far brother"** *(Proverbs 27:10).*

Solomon seems quite suspicious of fraternal loyalty. In several places he states that friends may be more reliable and helpful than brothers. But what about the saying, "Blood is thicker than water?"

The second of the above quotes may enlighten us about the first. Solomon was well aware of the emotions involved in relationships.

Two important factors that distinguish a friendship from a fraternal relationship. The first is that the family bond does not in any way dictate a commonality of ideas. Two brothers may be poles apart in thought and feeling. Friendships, on the other hand, usually come from sharing similar ideologies and goals. One brother may be very cautious, the other a risk taker. If the latter sustains a loss, the conservative brother may chastise his recklessness rather than sympathize with him. A friend, however, is someone who is probably of like mind — a risk taker. He will sympathize rather than chastise.

Secondly, we do not like to feel obligated. We will volunteer to do for others, but do not want to feel compelled to do so. A friend need not feel obligated. If he helps it is because he chooses to, and the help is wholehearted. A brother, however, precisely because "blood is thicker than water," may feel obligated to help. Obligation may give rise to resentment, and the help may be given grudgingly.

A wise person can lessen the feelings of obligation that a brother may have. This may allow the brother to give help freely and lovingly.

From Our
Heritage

NOTES

R' Sholom of Belz said that there are three varieties of exile, and they are of increasing severity.

One is when a Jew is in exile in a foreign land, subject to the oppression of strangers. The second is when a Jew is in exile by another Jew, oppressed by one of his own. This is far more distressing than being oppressed by a stranger.

Most difficult is when a person is in exile within himself. He is oppressed by his own person, and is not free to act as he wishes. Clinically, those suffering from an obsessive-compulsive disorder are tormented by feeling forced to do things they do not want to do.

We have some very strong internal drives. If they control us instead of us controlling them, we have lost our freedom. We are slaves to ourselves, in exile to ourselves. This is the most distressing exile of all.

"The end of a matter is better than its beginning" *(Ecclesiastes 7:8).*

July 31, 2004
Aug. 18, 2005

The Talmud offers another interpretation of this verse: "A good ending of a matter depends on its beginning" (Jerusalem Talmud *Chaggigah* 2:1). A project's inception affects its outcome.

The Torah repeatedly emphasizes "firsts." The first of the harvest is to be given to the *kohen*, the first-ripened fruits are to be brought as an offering, the first-born of animals are sacred, the first wool of the shearing is to be given to the *kohen*. We can invest everything with spiritual values, but we must set the pattern in the beginning.

Like many children over the centuries, I began to study Torah at age five, starting with *Leviticus*. My teacher explained that this *Book* describes the sacred offerings in the Temple, and when a child begins the study of Torah, it is as sacred as the service in the Temple.

The mother of R' Yehoshua ben Chananiah did better than that. She put his crib in the *beis midrash* so that the first sounds that entered the infant's mind would be those of Torah. Perhaps she knew then what is just coming to light now, that a mother's behavior can have a psychologic impact even on the unborn child.

What will happen to those infants whose ears and eyes are exposed to the most decadent speech and scenes when the parents leave them in the care of the babysitter, who entertains herself with the sordid programs on television? They may contend that the child cannot be affected by what it cannot possibly understand. R' Yehoshua ben Chananiah's mother knew better.

Wise parents will give their children a proper beginning.

From Our Heritage

The Baal Shem Tov often stressed the concept, "G-d desires the dedication of one's heart" (*Sanhedrin* 106b). There are many Chassidic stories that illustrate this.

R' Levi Yitzchak of Berditchev conducted his seder observing all the halachic and kabalistic details. In his dream he heard a message, "The seder of Chaim the water-carrier was superior to yours."

R' Levi Yitzchak sent for Chaim. "Tell me, Chaim, how did you conduct the seder?"

Chaim said, "I am really ashamed to tell you. Knowing that for eight days I will not be able to drink whisky, I drank heavily on *Erev Pesach.* My wife could not awaken me to conduct the seder. Finally, before dawn she succeeded in arousing me.

"'Chaim!,' she shouted, 'it's almost morning and you haven't made the seder!'

"I said, 'I know nothing about making a seder. All I know is that our ancestors were enslaved by the Gypsies and G-d liberated them. Now we are enslaved by the anti-Semitic despots that always make decrees against us. But just as G-d saved our ancestors, He will save us now. That's all I know!' And then I went back to sleep."

R' Levi Yitzchak said, "That was truly a great seder."

NOTES

AV

אב

Aug. 1, 2004
Aug. 19, 2005

From the Scriptures

"**I** shall not die! But I shall live and relate the deeds of G-d" *(Psalms 118:17).*

The words of this verse can also be read to mean, "I shall not die as long as I live." This can be thought of as a prayer to be able to live a full life to the very end, and not to fall victim to the dementing disease that may occur in advanced age. It can also be read as a declaration of determination: "I shall not allow any part of me to die as long as I live." It has been appropriately said that "the greatest loss is what dies inside us while we live."

When we are young we are ambitious and optimistic. We feel love and enthusiasm. As we grow older, we may be disappointed in not having realized some of our aspirations. This may cause us to lose our vitality.

At a crowded Chassidic gathering, I saw a ninety-three-year-old man deftly climb over a bench, pushing people aside to make room for himself. He said, "I am not an old man of ninety-three. I am three young men of thirty-one."

Our spirit is very much like our body. If we do not exercise and use our muscles, they atrophy and become weak. Failure to exercise our spirit causes similar atrophy.

It is tragic indeed to see elderly people who suffer from a disease which causes the brain to atrophy. Hopefully, scientific research will one day find a solution for this. But at this very moment we can prevent our spirit from wasting away. We should not allow ourselves to become dejected if we did not fulfill our aspirations. To the contrary, we can always have new spiritual aspirations.

Wise people keep their bodies young and healthy through proper nutrition and exercise. Really wise people do the same for the spirit.

From Our Heritage

NOTES

A *tzaddik* was sitting at the table surrounded by his students. "Which of you believes there is a G-d?" he asked.

The surprised students answered, "Rebbe, every day we say the *Shema* and declare that G-d is One."

"Perhaps you believe there is a G-d. I do not," the *tzaddik* said. Noting the astonishment of the students, the *tzaddik* asked, "Do you believe this is a table?'

The students replied, "We see the table right before us. We can touch it. We know it is there. There is no need to *believe* it is there."

"Exactly," the *tzaddik* said. "G-d's presence is so evident that I can see Him everywhere. There is no need for me to *believe*."

The popular aphorism, "Seeing is believing," is wrong. We only *believe* what we do not see. What we see we *know* exists.

"Do not look outside of yourself, and do not look into others." | *Words of Wisdom*

Aug. 2, 2004
Aug. 20, 2005

Chassidus teaches self-examination. We need take our own inventory, not that of other people.

The Baal Shem Tov taught that the world is a mirror, in which we see our own reflection. Since we are oblivious to our own defects, G-d shows them to us in others. "When you see a fault in another," the Baal Shem Tov said, "you should know that it is your own."

The Baal Shem Tov was uncompromising in this. He once happened to see someone violate Shabbos. He did an intensive soul-searching to discover where he had violated Shabbos. He was convinced that had he not been guilty of violating Shabbos, he would not have seen this. When he failed to find how he had violated Shabbos, he prayed that it be revealed to him. He found that the *Zohar* states that a Torah scholar has the sanctity of Shabbos. He had once heard a disparaging comment about a Torah scholar and did not repudiate it. This was tantamount to a violation of Shabbos.

What a different world it would be if we implemented the Baal Shem Tov's teaching! In the introductory prayer composed by R' Elimelech of Lizhensk he says, "Help me to see the virtues of other people and not their faults." As with everything else, G-d will give us the help we need, but we must initiate the process.

The Talmud relates that two people passed a carcass. One commented on the foul odor it emanated. The other said, "Look at the whiteness of its teeth!"

A wise person will expend his energies finding things within himself that need improvement and go about doing it.

From Our Heritage

At Sinai, "The entire assembly of Israelites declared *in unison,* 'all that G-d says we shall do'" (*Exodus* 19:8). R' Meir Simcha of Dvinsk asked, "How could everyone promise to fulfill *all* of G-d's commandments? There are some things which one may not be able to do. An Israelite cannot do those *mitzvos* that are unique for a *kohen.* If a person's first child is a girl, he cannot fulfill the *mitzvah* of *pidyon haben* (redemption of the first born son)."

R' Meir Simcha answered, "When a person gives *tzedakah,* it is not the hand that has the *mitzvah,* but the whole person. When a person eats the matzah, it is not the mouth that has the *mitzvah,* but the whole person. All parts of the body are one. Anything performed by one part of the body is ascribed to the entire body.

"So it is with *mitzvos.* When Jews are united, they are like a single body. The Israelite participates in the *mitzvos* of a *kohen.* The father of a first-born girl shares in the *mitzvah* of one who has a *pidyon haben.* It was because the Israelites were united and responded *in unison* that they could promise to each fulfill *all* of G-d's commandments."

NOTES

_____

_____

_____

_____

_____

_____

_____

_____

AV

אב

Aug. 3, 2004
Aug. 21, 2005

From the Sages

"**T**his is the way of Torah: Eat bread with salt, drink water in small measure, sleep on the ground...If you do this you will be fortunate in both this world and in the World to Come"
(Ethics of the Fathers 6:4).

How fortunate can one be in this world if one lives so frugally? Some explain this to mean that if you can adapt to an austere life, you will always be content with what you have. If you need more than the basics, you may not be content no matter what you have.

It has been wisely said that one of humanity's problems is that luxuries can quickly become necessities.

After World War II, many Holocaust survivors came to Israel. They were totally destitute. Our congregation gathered used clothing to send them. One thank you letter we received was *written on personal stationery.* I was flabbergasted, and said to my father, "This woman has no clothes of her own, yet she has personal stationery!"

My father told me that he recognized the woman's name. She came from a family that had been wealthy. Personal stationery was as basic to her as having food and clothing. She had no concept that this was a luxury, and that many people did not have personal stationery. Although she had lost everything in the Holocaust, her concept of what constitutes the necessities of life had not changed.

Indeed, the Torah requires that, in giving *tzedakah,* the recipient's previous standard of living be considered. A person accustomed to extras should be given money for them (*Rashi Deuteronomy* 15:8).

That should be our attitude to others. As for ourselves, a wise person will take caution not to allow luxuries to become necessities.

From Our Heritage

Moses Montefiore was once sitting at the Shabbos table when a messenger came from a lord with whom Montefiore did much business. The nobleman requested Montefiore to promptly come to his home. There was an opportunity to make a deal with huge profits, but it had to be sealed immediately. Montefiore told the man that he could not conduct business on the Sabbath, and sent him back.

The messenger soon returned. His master said it was urgent that Montefiore come at once. He would not have to do anything, but his presence was mandatory. Again Montefiore refused.

The messenger returned a third time, with a letter from the lord. The messenger read it aloud. It sharply stated that if he did not come promptly he would be held responsible for losing this profit and the nobleman would no longer do any business with him.

Montefiore sent his regrets, thanking the lord for his many favors, and explaining that he could not comply with his present wish.

After Shabbos the lord told Montefiore that there was never a deal. Another nobleman had said that Jews are so money hungry that they would sell their religion for money. "I wagered that you would not. I am grateful that you enabled me to be triumphant."

"All beginnings are difficult" (Rashi Exodus 19:5).

From the Sages

Many good things remain undone because there is difficulty in getting them started. Inertia is a powerful deterrent. A heavy box may be difficult to move, but once someone begins to move it, it is much easier to push it along. With many projects there are people who are willing to help, provided that someone else initiates them.

There is a Yiddish aphorism, "The appetite comes with the eating." How many times have you said, "I'm not hungry, but I'll sit at the table with you." Then you take a nibble of something, perhaps consent to eat the appetizer, and before you know it, you have eaten a whole meal.

Many people have told me that they have an idea for a book. "How do you go about writing a book?" they ask. My answer is, "You start!" Once you begin, it develops its own momentum.

It is not necessary to wait for inspiration. I doubt that Beethoven or Mozart waited for inspiration. I suspect that they sat down with only one idea: to write music. They did not compose because they were inspired. Rather, the inspiration came with the composition. I suspect that many a time they sat down with a melody playing in their minds and then wrote something else altogether! My own experience has been similar. I am often surprised that what I ended up writing bears little similarity to the idea with which I began.

Wise people know that there is an inertia that they must overcome if they want to get something done. They do not wait for someone else to initiate it.

Aug. 4, 2004
Aug. 22, 2005

From Our Heritage

The Talmud has high praises for people who underwent great sacrifice to honor their parents. R' Aryeh Levin tells of a contemporary incident.

A young man devoted much time and energy helping his father develop his vineyard to a flourishing success. After he married, he left home. His younger brother, who had never invested any effort in the vineyard, manipulated the father to give him sole title to it.

When the older brother became aware of this, he asked his father why he had deprived him of his share in the vineyard, particularly since he had put so much work into its development. The father said, "I guess I didn't realize what I was doing. You know, my mind isn't what it used to be. Your brother came with a very shrewd lawyer, and before I knew it, I had signed the papers.

"It is not fair to deprive you. I will make a declaration that I was not in my right mind at the time, and that will nullify the deal."

"You will do no such thing," the son said. "I will forfeit the property before I allow you to declare that you were not of sound mind!"

When R' Aryeh Levin related this story, he said, "I so envy this man for the great *mitzvah* he had of sacrificing his inheritance to preserve his father's dignity."

NOTES

From the Scriptures

"Whence shall come wisdom?" *(Job 28:12)*

These words lend themselves to another translation as well, this one a statement: "Wisdom shall emerge from nothingness."

The Baal Shem Tov was asked how we know that the path of *chassidus* is correct. The Baal Shem answered, "A man was lost in the forest. He came upon another person and asked, 'Could you show me the way out of the forest?' The second man answered, 'No, I too am looking for the way out. But I marked off paths that do not lead out of the forest, so we know which to avoid.'"

People who have a spouse, sibling, or child with a drug or alcohol problem ask me how they should relate to them. I tell them to attend meetings of family groups of chemically dependent people. One immediate benefit in meeting with people with experience is learning what *not* to do. These people have tried techniques that were futile. Why make your own mistakes when you can learn from someone else's? I am surprised that some people reject the recommendation, and make the very mistakes they could have avoided.

Wisdom may come from nothingness. I.e., there can be a negative approach to knowing how to live. That is by avoiding the ways which do *not* lead us to our goal. But this presupposes that we have a goal. You cannot look for a path if you do not have a destination.

Luzzato begins his epochal *Path of the Just* by examining what a person's goal in life should be. He then provides a ten step program to reach that goal. He employs a dual approach, advising what one should do and what pitfalls one should avoid.

Wise people decide what they wish to do with their lives. By observing methods that clearly do not lead to their goal, they know paths to avoid. This makes finding the right path so much easier.

From Our Heritage

One of the greatest *mitzvos* of *gemilas chassadim* (acts of kindness) is to gladden the hearts of widows, orphans, and the downtrodden. This was the outstanding feature of R' Aryeh Levin, whose dedication to *chesed* took him to visit even the social castaways in prison.

Doing *chesed* requires thoughtfulness and sensitivity. On *Chol Hamoed* (the intermediate days of *Pesach* and *Succos*), R' Aryeh would take one or more friends and visit the widows of the late Torah scholars. He explained, "During the work week, people are occupied with their business. On Shabbos there is no transportation. On *Chol Hamoed* people are free from work, and that is when they customarily visit their teachers and Torah leaders.

"When the Torah scholars were alive, their homes would buzz with activity on *Chol Hamoed*. This is the time when their widows feel their loss most deeply and experience the terrible loneliness."

R' Aryeh's greatness was not only in doing *chesed*, but in his sensitivity in knowing what needed to be done.

NOTES

_____
_____
_____
_____
_____
_____
_____
_____
_____

"You are very wise in that you heed the words of the Torah scholars" *(Negaim 9:3).*

From the Sages

We have Torah scholars and spiritual leaders. We may indeed ask them for halachic decisions. However, we do not often ask their advice about how we should become more spiritual.

A chassidic rebbe told one of his *chassidim* that he must set aside time for Torah study and spend more time *davening* (praying). The *chassid* explained that his business is so demanding that he cannot find the time. The rebbe said, "Is it not strange? People come for my advice about buying a house, going into a business, or making a *shidduch* (a marriage match). I do not have any expertise in these. But when I tell them how they must become more spiritual, which *is* my area of expertise, they do not listen."

Perhaps we do not ask our Torah scholars how to become more spiritual because we do not wish to hear what they will tell us.

R' Yitzchak Meir of Gur was an outstanding Torah scholar whose works on Talmud testify to his extraordinary brilliance. He wrote a commentary on the *Shulchan Aruch Choshen Mishpat* (the laws of commerce and damages) and showed it to R' Mendel of Kotzk, the erstwhile colleague whom he had accepted as his rebbe.

R' Mendel reviewed the work and said, "It is excellent, but its excellence is its fault. If this is published, scholars will study your commentary instead of the accepted commentary of the *Shach.* That should not be allowed to happen. Throw it into the fire."

R' Yitzchak Meir did not hesitate. He took the work over which he had labored for so long , said, "I am fulfilling the *mitzvah* of obeying the words of scholars (*Yevamos* 20a)," and tossed it into the fire.

Wise people ask for, and follow, the guidance of Torah scholars.

From Our Heritage

R' Moshe Schreiber (author of *Chasam Sofer*) collected money to help needy families. One winter day he knocked on the door of a wealthy man who rarely parted with his money. The man invited the rabbi into his house, but R' Moshe remained standing at the door.

R' Moshe explained his mission, that he was raising money to help the poor, and that he was asking for a substantial donation. The man was shivering in the cold and said, "Rabbi, please come into the house. I will be glad to give you *tzedakah.*"

R' Moshe said, "No, I prefer to transact with you right here, where you can feel what it is like to be in the cold. You will soon enter your warm house, and you may have little sympathy for those families who cannot afford wood for the fire. Here in the cold you may better understand their suffering and not dispense me with a pittance."

Yesterday we read about R' Aryeh Levin's extraordinary sensitivity in understanding people's needs. Those who are not sensitive may have to be helped to be sensitive.

NOTES

Aug. 7, 2004
Aug. 25, 2005

From the Sages

"**W**hat you are needed for should be of greater concern to you than what you need" *(R' Shneur Zalman of Liadi).*

This comment was made by the author of *Tanya* to a *chassid* who complained to the rebbe about his many problems. The rebbe was by no means indifferent to the *chassid's* difficulties and did indeed help him. However, his remark was valid. The *chassid* was so overwhelmed with his problems that he had lost sight of contemplating about his obligations in the world.

It has been said that great minds have purposes, others have wishes.

One of the unique traits that distinguish human beings from other forms of life is that animals have no concept of doing things other than for themselves. People can conceptualize a purpose in life beyond the self.

R' Mendel of Kotzk asked R' Yaakov of Radzimin what he feels is the purpose of a person's existence. "To achieve *tikun* (rectification) for the *neshamah* (soul)," R' Yaakov answered.

"That is not what we learned in Pschis'che," R' Mendel said. "The purpose of man's existence is to elevate the glory of G-d."

It would appear that *tikun* of the *neshamah* is a very spiritual goal. R' Mendel was not satisfied with this. Even though it is highly spiritual, it is one's own *neshamah* that one is rectifying, and this makes it a self-directed purpose. This is what R' Mendel meant with his comment on the statement in *Ethics of the Fathers* (2:17), "All your deeds should be for the sake of Heaven." R' Mendel said, "Even your 'for the sake of Heaven deeds' should be for the sake of Heaven." Some deeds can be very spiritual, yet be essentially self directed.

A wise person knows that inasmuch as fulfillment of one's purpose is a component of happiness, one cannot be truly happy unless he searches beyond himself.

From Our Heritage

NOTES

_____
_____
_____
_____
_____
_____
_____
_____

During the years R' Chaim Soloveitchek was rabbi in Brisk, the community covered his household expenses, including firewood for heat. When they reviewed the bills at the end of the year, they found that the expense for firewood was inordinately high. A bit of research revealed that the firewood bin was not locked, and the poor of the city would help themselves. They had a lock placed on the bin and gave the key to the *shammas.*

When R' Chaim discovered this, he ordered the lock removed. The community officials told him that there was not enough money in the community coffers to supply all the poor with firewood

R' Chaim said, "If so, then my house, too, will remain unheated. I cannot sit in a warm house when I know that the poor are freezing."

"I despised the labor which I labored under the sun, for I shall leave it to a man who shall succeed me. And who knows whether he will be a wise man or a fool? Yet he will rule over all the wealth for which I labored" *(Ecclesiastes 2:18-19).*

Aug. 8, 2004
Aug. 26, 2005

These are very sobering words. A father may leave the wealth which he worked so hard to accumulate to a son who may use it destructively. Yet, for whom did he labor all those years if not for his son? The thought that he sacrificed so much to amass wealth, and yet it may be used destructively by a foolish heir, is very depressing.

Did Solomon suspect that his son Rechabam would reject the wise counsel of the elders and follow his friends' foolish advice, causing ten tribes to secede from the kingdom and bring it to ruin?

What does this teach us? First, that though we want to provide our children with comfort, we must not sacrifice everything toward this end. We should devote proper time to satisfy our spiritual needs. We should set aside time for Torah study, and devote enough time so that our prayers are truly heartfelt. While we wish to provide for a child, let us remember that we, too, are someone's child.

Secondly, parents should not deceive themselves about their children. If a child has shown that he uses money irresponsibly, it is not a kindness to provide him with the means for self-destruction. In such a case, the estate should be left in trust, with allotments given to the child according to the discretion of the trustees.

Wise children use their inheritance wisely. Foolish children not only dissipate the father's wealth, but also fail to develop a skill with which to earn a living. When the inheritance has been squandered, they are worse off than if their father had left them nothing.

Late one Friday night, R' Aryeh Levin heard a knock on the door. He opened it to find a man desperate for his advice. His wife had suffered a relapse of mental illness, and refused to be go to the hospital unless the rabbi agrees she should do so. R' Aryeh told him to tell his wife that he insists that she immediately go to the hospital, and that he wishes her a *refuah sheleimah* (full recovery). "You've saved my life!" the man exclaimed, and quickly ran from the house.

The following morning R' Aryeh told his grandson the incident and said, "Look how dear truth is to this man. He walked several miles to my home. He could have walked around the block a few times and told his wife that I had approved of her hospitalization. She would have believed him. But he did not want to tell a lie.

"We must learn from this man. Even when he was in so dire a predicament, he refused to lie, and went to such great lengths to avoid it. This man truly observed the Torah *mitzvah*, 'Distance yourself from falsehood'" *(Exodus* 23:7).

From Our Heritage

NOTES

Aug. 9, 2004
Aug. 27, 2005

From the Sages

"A person who thinks poorly of himself because he is unaware of his strengths is not humble; he is a fool"** *(R' Yehudah Leib Chasman).*

When I came across this quote from this noted ethicist, I was elated. It validated what I wrote in *Let Us Make Man*—that self-esteem is not *ga'avah* (vanity). I took this a step further. Self-esteem is being aware of one's personality assets. Without such awareness one cannot have *anivus* (humility). Indeed, *ga'avah* is the *antitheses* of self-esteem; it is a defensive reaction to a feeling of low self-worth. How thrilled I was to find this very concept stated by no less an authority than the great Rabbeinu Yonah. "The person who thinks of himself as great is trying to find relief from painful feelings of low self-worth!" *(Rabbeinu Yonah al HaTorah)*

It has been aptly stated that *our beliefs about what we are and what we can be precisely determine what we will be.*

R' Aharon of Karlin said that though dejection is not explicitly a sin, "there is nothing so conducive to sin as dejection." He was not referring to appropriate grief, such as when one, G-d forbid, loses a loved one, or when we mourn the loss of the Temple. The dejection he denounces is a feeling of inferiority and worthlessness. This is nothing other than a tool the *yetzer hara* uses to disable a person.

Awareness of one's abilities and talents places an obligation on the person to perform commensurately. One of the most annoying statements may be, "You have such great potential." Some people would feel more comfortable if they had less potential. They would not have to make any demands of themselves.

The feeling, "I am great" is *ga'avah.* The feeling, "I am able *to be great"* is the antithesis of *ga'avah*, because it leads to, "If I have the capacity to be great, why am I not exercising it?" That is *anivus.*

A wise person avoids the appellation of being the fool R' Yehudah Leib Chasman describes.

From Our Heritage

NOTES

_____
_____
_____
_____
_____
_____
_____

Some people take precautions not to write dates as 2/18/01, because this designates January as being the first month and February the second, and the Torah states that Nissan is the first month (*Exodus* 12:2).

Baron Shimon Rothschild felt this way. He once engaged a *sofer* (scribe) to write *tefillin*, mezuzos, and the *megillos.* When the *sofer* delivered the finished products, Rothschild asked him to list any payments on account. The *sofer* took out his notebook and showed him that he had received payments on 4/25, 6/12, and 7/18.

Baron Rothschild paid the *sofer* the balance due him and said, "Take the *tefillin,* mezuzos, and the *megillos* with you. I am not interested in sacred writings that were written by someone who violates the Torah designation of Nissan as being the first month."

"The Talmud says that we should always judge other people favorably. We must also judge ourselves favorably" *(R' Nachman of Breslav).*

AV

23

אב

Aug. 10, 2004
Aug. 28, 2005

From the Sages

This is a continuation of yesterday's theme. R' Nachman's words must be properly understood. Taken out of context, they appear to be incompatible with the teachings of *mussar,* which requires that we examine ourselves thoroughly to detect our faults. If we judge ourselves favorably, might we not find rationalizations whereby to justify our errant behavior rather than correct it?

R' Nachman is saying that one who has done wrong is at risk of feeling so down that he may despair of *teshuvah.* He should, therefore, try to judge himself favorably and find merits within himself. A person may have a garment which is so thoroughly soiled that it cannot be cleaned. On the other hand, a fine garment that has a stain can be cleaned and restored to beauty. If an errant person sees himself as fundamentally good, he will not become hopeless, but he will try to correct himself to be the good person he can be.

R' Nachman describes times when he felt terribly depressed, almost beyond hope. It was at times like these that he thought of the verse, "If I ascend to Heaven, You are there. And if I make my bed in the nethermost depths, You are there, too" *(Psalms* 139:8). A person may feel that he has fallen so far away from G-d that he is beyond redemption. He must know that wherever he is, G-d is near.

The *tzaddik* of Sanz used to say, "I promise You, G-d, that I will try to be good. I know that I said this yesterday and did not carry out my promise. But today I really mean it."

Wise people judge themselves favorably not to excuse their mistakes, but to realize that they have the ability to correct them.

From Our Heritage

NOTES

R' Levi Yitzchak was collecting money for the poor and felt he would have more success if another respected person came along. He asked a Torah scholar to accompany him. The latter responded, "Gladly. As soon as I finish my daily portion of *Tehillim (Psalms).*"

R' Levi Yitzchak said, "The poor are hungry and cold, and you want them to wait until you finish your *Tehillim*? G-d has thousands of angels who sing His praises far better than you do. Not one of them can give a hungry person a piece of bread."

R' Levi Yitzchak's granddaughter married the son of R' Shneur Zalman (author of *Tanya*). After the wedding, R' Levi Yitzchak said to R' Shneur Zalman, "G-d has been gracious, enabling us to marry off our children. Let us thank Him by doing a *mitzvah* together."

"Certainly," R' Shneur Zalman said. "What do you suggest?"

"Let us collect money for *hachnassas kallah* (covering wedding expenses for needy couples)."

And they did.

Aug. 11, 2004
Aug. 29, 2005

From the Sages

"**E**verything is in the hands of G–d, except for reverence of G–d" *(Berachos 33b).*

This is the way the Talmud expresses the concept of *bechirah* (freedom of choice). G-d has left the choice between right and wrong entirely up to people. He does not intervene to stop a person from doing wrong.

Bechirah is the crown jewel of mankind. Neither angels nor animals can choose. Angels must do what they are assigned. Animals do what their body desires. Only man is free to do as he wishes.

Freedom of choice is a Divine gift. It has been said that G-d gave people two incredible gifts: awesome abilities and freedom of choice. It is tragic that too often man rejects both.

Some philosophers and psychologists have denied that man has freedom of choice. They claim that the latter is but an illusion. A computerized robot may appear to have the ability to choose. Actually, it is only doing what has been programmed into it. It cannot initiate choice. They say this is true of man as well.

There is an appeal to this type of thinking. When Job could not explain why he was made to suffer, he concluded that all of a person's actions are determined and are not the result of free choice. In this way, Job was able to shed any responsibility for what happened to him. There is comfort in being able to avoid responsibility.

Sometimes a person may surrender his freedom of choice. He may allow himself to be controlled by his body, friends, or environment. Children sometimes say, "He made me do it!"

Only two beings have freedom of choice: G-d and man. This is what was meant that man was created "in the likeness of G-d" *(Genesis* 1:27). Wise people prize this identity. Only a fool would surrender it.

From Our Heritage

NOTES

"If the opportunity to do a mitzvah presents itself, do not delay it" *(Rashi, Exodus* 12:17).

Shimon Nathaniel Rothschild of Frankfurt was once approached in the street by a man who related his desperate circumstances. Rothschild was moved by this person's plight and wanted to help him, but did not have any money with him at the time. He removed the gold chain from his watch and gave it to the man.

The man was taken by surprise. "Heaven forbid!" he said. "I cannot take your gold chain. I am so grateful that you wish to help me. I will come to your office tomorrow."

"No, no," Rothschild said. "Right now I feel for you. Who knows whether I will have the same feelings tomorrow? Does not Solomon say, 'Do not tell someone, "Come back later and I will give you" when you have the means to do so now?' " *(Proverbs* 3:28).

We should not lose the feeling of fervor for a *mitzvah.*

"Mitzvos require *kavannah* (concentration)" *(Berachos 13a).*

There is a legend that someone asked Satan what was his most potent tool to cause people to sin. Lust? Falsehood? Greed? Envy? Satan answered, "None of these. My most effective tool is apathy."

In Torah literature, *kavannah* occupies a central place, "Prayer without *kavannah* is like a lifeless body" (*Introduction to R' Yaakov of Emden Siddur*). This is equally true of all *mitzvos.*

A rebbe expounded on the theme of "Know G–d in all your ways" (*Proverbs* 3:6), saying that it is not enough to think about G–d when doing *mitzvos.* A person should dedicate everything he does to G–d and constantly think of Him. One *chassid* said, "Is it realistic to expect me to think about G–d when I am transacting business?" The rebbe answered, "Why not? You seem to have no difficulty thinking about business when you are *davening* (praying)."

A lecturer to a group of business executives said, "If you think of your golf game while showering, your business will suffer." Success in business requires total commitment. The litmus test of the quality of commitment toward anything is how much the person thinks about it when he is away from it.

Commitment and apathy are polar opposites. A person who is apathetic about something will drop it at the first hint of failure. A committed person presses on and on. "A righteous person may fall seven times but will arise" (*Proverbs* 24:16).

A wise person decides what is most important to him and commits himself to it.

A woman came to R' Aharon of Karlin with a tale of woe. She was a widow with little earnings. In order to do a *shidduch* (marriage match) with her daughter, she had promised a dowry. The wedding date was approaching, and if she does not deliver on her promise, the wedding will be called off. R' Aharon inquired how much she needed, and gave her the entire amount.

Several days later the woman returned, explaining that she did not have a proper dress for the wedding, and would be embarrassed not to be dressed appropriately. R' Aharon reflected for a few moments, then gave her money for a dress.

R' Aharon's wife said, "I understand giving her money to avoid the wedding being cancelled. But why give her money for a dress? Surely the wedding would go on even if she did not have the dress. It would have been better to give that money to other poor people."

R' Aharon answered, "That thought occurred to me as well. I reflected, 'Whose suggestion is it that I give the money to other poor people? The *yetzer tov* or the *yetzer hara?*' I concluded that inasmuch as I had this money for the past two days and the *yetzer tov* did not tell me to give it to the poor, this suggestion must be that of the *yetzer hara.* That is why I gave her the money."

Aug. 12, 2004
Aug. 30, 2005

From Our Heritage

NOTES

AV

אב

Aug. 13, 2004
Aug. 31, 2005

From the Scriptures

"G-d gives wisdom; from His mouth are knowledge and understanding" *(Proverbs 2:6).*

In his essay on the intellect, R' Avraham Grodzinski states that a person is held responsible not only for failure to apply the intellect he has, but also for failure to apply the full intellect *he could have had* if he had developed his intellectual potential to its maximum.

R' Avraham notes that the generation of the flood and the people of Sodom and Gommorah did not violate any explicit Divine commandments, for they had none. But they behaved in a way their intellect, *had they utilized it to its fullest,* dictated as wrong.

Sodom and Gommorah had laws, but the laws were morally corrupt. A well-developed intellect would have shown this up.

This is relevant today. Frank abominations are permitted to corrupt our population and particularly our youth. Graphic violence has become entertaining. These practices are protected by the First Amendment. The lives of many young people are being destroyed by a drug epidemic, because purveyors of these poisons are allowed to remain at large as a result of the existing criminal justice system. Outrageous miscarriages of justice are not uncommon, and are sanctioned by the legal system. These laws are the product of human intellect, but it is an intellect that has been stunted. A fully developed intellect would never permit sanction of these atrocities.

R' Avraham states that just as a judge who accepts a bribe cannot judge fairly, neither can an intellect develop fully if a person is "bribed" by desires whose gratification would be prohibited by a fully developed intellect.

A truly wise person will not assume that his intellect is at his maximum. He will continue to develop his intellect, regardless of what personal inconvenience this may cost.

From Our Heritage

The rebbe of Amshinov once asked a wealthy man for *tzedakah* to help a relative of the latter who had fallen upon hard times.

"He is a distant relative," the wealthy man said. "I hardly know him. I don't feel that I have any special obligation toward him."

"Did you *daven* (pray) this morning?" the rebbe asked.

"Of course I *davened,*" the man answered.

"What was the opening paragraph of the *Amidah*?"

"Everyone knows that," the man answered. "The G-d of Abraham, Isaac, and Jacob."

"When did they live?" the rebbe asked.

"Several thousand years ago," the man answered.

"You asked G-d to be kind to you because of the merits of ancestors that lived thousands of years ago and are very, very, distant from you. Yet you deny kindness to a contemporary relative because he is distant. How do you think G-d will respond to your prayer?"

NOTES

"Blessed is G-d who fashioned the human being with wisdom" *(blessing after personal care).*

Aug. 14, 2004
Sept. 1, 2005

This blessing can be fully understood only if one knows the physiology of the human being. All the wonders of the world pale into nothingness in comparison to the exquisite function of the human body. Yet, we take this all for granted.

The precision of regulatory systems within the human body stagger the imagination. Sitting at the base of the brain is the tiny pituitary gland, no larger than a thumbnail, which analyzes the level of the various hormones in the body and controls their production by the various glands. The chemical process carried out by the liver could not be duplicated even by a fully computerized chemical laboratory complex spread over several acres.

Even our limited knowledge of the function of the brain leaves one as breathless as seeing the majesty of Victoria Falls. Virtually every move made by a person requires the sending and registering of virtually *millions* of messages within the central nervous system. Compared to the complexity of the brain, the most advanced computer in the world is nothing more than a tinker toy.

A physician specializing in infertility said, "I was once peering through the microscope at a fertilized ovum. I realized that from this point on, this single tiny cell will only receive nutrients, out of which it will fashion a full human being that can see, hear, speak, think, and compose great masterpieces. A that moment I realized that there must be a G-d!"

"From my flesh I can see G-d" *(Job* 19:26). A wise person will concentrate on the above blessing and stand in awe of the Divine wisdom.

When R' Nosson Tzvi Finkel was at a health resort, he was observed spending much time with an elderly person. He was overheard to be impressing the man with the importance of Torah. Just as the a human being is lifeless without a *neshamah*, so is the Jewish nation lifeless without Torah. It was assumed that R' Nosson Tzvi hoped to convince this man to support the yeshivah.

It turned out that the man was from an irreligious home and knew little about *Yiddishkeit.* He was poor, in ill health, and depended on meager support provided by his children. When asked why he spent so much time with this man, R' Nosson Tzvi replied:

"This man is in the twilight of his life. In actuality, he can do nothing to support of Torah. But if he understands the importance of Torah, he would *want* to support Torah. The will is itself meritorious. How tragic it would be for him to live his life without any merits!"

How important it is to try and give every person a *zechus* (merit)!

From Our Heritage

NOTES

_____
_____
_____
_____
_____
_____
_____
_____
_____

AV

אב

Aug. 15, 2004
Sept. 2, 2005

*From
the
Scriptures*

"**L**et him who is wise take note and the loving-kindnesses of G-d will make themselves understood"** *(Psalms 107:43).*

This psalm describes four types of peril which people may encounter, and the gratitude they should express to G-d when they emerge safely. These are (1) travelers who are lost in the wilderness, (2) people who have been in captivity, (3) people who suffered serious illness, and (4) survivors of near shipwreck.

One might ask, "Why put me into a perilous state and then save me? Why not just avoid the peril?"

We are much like a totally deaf person who enters a concert hall. He may not understand why a person who is standing on the stage is gesturing wildly to a group of people who are manipulating strange instruments and why hundreds of people rise and clap their hands. All this makes sense only if one can hear the music.

Why people are put into precarious states is beyond our understanding. We cannot "hear the music." We should have faith that there is design in what transpires.

The Baal Shem Tov instituted that *Psalm* 107 should be recited before we greet Shabbos. It is rare that a week goes by that we did not experience things which made us think, "Why me?"

Shabbos is a testimony to creation. The universe did not just happen to come into being by some freak accident. In the Friday-night *kiddush* we assert our belief that G-d created the world. In His infinite wisdom, there is reason for everything. With our limited intellect we cannot hope to grasp this. However, we can be wise enough to understand that in G-d's infinite goodness, there is a benign purpose to everything.

The fool will look upon the adversities that occur and may deny G-d or attribute improper motives to Him. The wise will accept the vicissitudes of life with faith in the benevolence of G-d.

*From Our
Heritage*

NOTES

R' Nachman of Breslav stood at the window and saw Chaikel moving about frenetically in the marketplace. He beckoned to him. "Chaikel," he said, "have you looked up to the heavens today?"

"No," Chaikel said. "I am very busy."

"Come here, Chaikel," R' Nachman said. "Tell me what you see."

"I see horses, wagons, and people running to-and-fro."

"Ay, Chaikel, Chaikel," R' Nachman said. "Fifty years from now there will be a market here, but with different participants. There will be different horses, different wagons, and different people. You and I will not be here. Yet, you are so preoccupied with everything so ephemeral that you do not have even a single moment to contemplate on what is permanent!"

Are we not all like Chaikel?

"A poor, wise lad is better than an old, foolish king" *(Ecclesiastes 4:13).*

Erev Rosh Chodesh
[Eve of the New Month]

Aug. 16, 2004
Sept. 3, 2005

The Midrash says that the "old, foolish king" refers to the *yetzer hara.* R' Yisrael of Rizhin said, "I never understood this. That the *yetzer hara* is old is true. It is old as creation. That it is a king is true, because it rules over so many people. But a fool? Hardly. To the contrary, it appears to be very clever and shrewd, finding devious ways to snare people.

"But when I was imprisoned I realized that the *yetzer hara* is indeed a fool, because there it was in prison, right with me! I said, 'You fool! I had no choice. They took me to prison in chains. But you came here of your own accord. You are indeed a fool!' "

R' Yisrael's point is that the *yetzer hara* is relentless. It never gives up, hence one must always be on guard.

A *chassid* who was in his last moments of life said to those surrounding him, "I have the urge to say the *Shema* with great *kavannah* (concentration). This is nothing but a ruse by the *yetzer hara* to trap me into *ga'avah* (vanity) in the last moments of my life, so that people will say of me 'What a *tzaddik*! He died with the *Shema* on his lips.' "

When the Baal Shem Tov was dying, his disciples saw his lips moving. They bent down and heard that he was saying, "Do not bring me to the brink of *ga'avah*" *(Psalms* 36:12).

A wise person will remember that he must always be on guard against the wile of the *yetzer hara.*

From Our Heritage

A visitor from Eretz Yisrael came to R' Naftali Tzvi Berlin *(Netziv).* R' Naftali extended him a warm welcome, and inquired about how things were in the Holy Land.

The visitor sighed. "Spirituality in Eretz Yisrael has suffered a severe decline. It is not at all like it was in previous generations."

R' Naftali arose and said angrily, "Stop! I do not wish to hear anything derogatory about Eretz Yisrael."

The guest said, "Believe me, Rabbi, I am not distorting the facts. What I am telling you is the truth."

R' Naftali said, "The spies that Moses sent did not lie either. They accurately described what they saw. Yet, it was their derogatory talk about the Holy Land that led to the calamity from which we suffer even today. If you cannot speak favorably about Eretz Yisrael, then say nothing!"

NOTES

**First Day of
Rosh Chodesh
Elul**

*Aug. 17, 2004
Sept. 4, 2005*

*Words
of
Wisdom*

"Listen, my child, to the *mussar* of your father, and do not forsake the teachings of your mother" *(Proverbs 1:8).*

Parents desire that their children be upright and decent. Then try to teach them principles of good conduct.

It is important to realize that lecturing to children is not very effective. Children are much more apt to do what they see their parents *do* than what they tell them to do.

Children learn respect when they see respect. If father and mother speak respectfully to each other and show that they honor each other, the children are likely to adopt this attitude. If parents avoid speaking *lashon* hara (gossip) and say, "Let's stop the conversation right here. We shouldn't be saying bad things about anyone," then the children are more apt to avoid *lashon hara* (gossip) and say, "Let's stop the conversation right here. We shouldn't be saying bad things about anyone," then the children are more apt to avoid *lashon hara*. If parents are careful to say "thank you" to each other and to the children, the latter learn to express gratitude.

Parents are upset when their children do no obey them. Children should be taught to defer to authority. If parents criticize the teacher, principal, or rabbi in front of the children, they undermine the children's respect not only for these authorities, but their own authority as well. Differences of opinion with other individuals of authority should be discussed with those people. It is also very important that parents show children how they themselves defer to authority.

Parents want their children to respect truth. They should be very careful to avoid all shades of falsehood themselves.

The *mussar* of the father and the teachings of the mother are conveyed most effectively by action rather than words.

*From Our
Heritage*

R' Yaakov Yosef once met a young man in the court of the Baal Shem Tov, who appeared to be in deep meditation. "*Shalom aleichem,*" R' Yaakov Yosef said. "*Aleichem shalom,*" the man responded.

NOTES

"Where do you come from?" R' Yaakov Yosef asked.

"Don't bother me now," the young man said, "what difference is it to you where I'm from?"

R' Yaakov Yosef said, "It is traditional that when two Jews meet, they exchange information about themselves. That is the beginning of a relationship. They may discover that they can be of help to one another. When they meet again, the relationship is reinforced. They become closer, and an affection develops.

"When Jews become closer to one another, it gives G-d great joy, just as when a father sees that his children have a close relationship.

"Your meditation is very important, but it should not preclude your developing closeness with fellow Jews."

"**A** requisite for acquisition of Torah is recognizing one's place" *(Ethics of the Fathers 6:6).*

Second Day of Rosh Chodesh

Aug. 18, 2004
Sept. 5, 2005

This has given rise to the aphorism, "Who is a wise person? One who recognizes his place."

Have you ever come to an event with assigned seats and were disappointed because you had expected to be seated "more prominently?" It seems that whoever arranged the seating thought more highly of other people than of you. This insult may have ruined your evening.

In several of my books, I discuss the importance of self-esteem. Not vanity, but the knowledge that you are worthy and likeable. With self-esteem, you need no external validation. You do not need to be seated near the front so others see that you are important. You can be seated anywhere and fully enjoy the evening.

But, you may say, feeling that way about myself *is* vanity, is it not?

What does the Talmud say? The Talmud condemns vanity, stating that though G–d rests His spirit among sinners (*Leviticus* 16:16), He absents Himself from a vain person (*Arachin* 15b). Nonetheless, the Talmud says, "The place a person occupies does not honor him. Rather, the person honors the place he occupies" (*Taanis* 21a). The Talmud that denounces vanity suggests that a person should feel, "Wherever I happen to be sitting is an honorable place."

I recall the *beis midrash* of R' Meir of Amshinov in Jerusalem. He did not have a prominent seat in front. His humility, and his greatness, were genuine. Wherever he was, was a place of honor.

When you were making seating arrangements for an affair, you undoubtedly said, "We have to seat Mr. X. up front, or we'll never hear the end of it." Did you think highly of Mr. X.? Do you want other people to think that way about you?

A wise person is one who knows his place. It is any place.

From Our Heritage

NOTES

Two litigants came to a rabbi for a *din Torah* (trial). They each claimed rights to some land between their two properties. Neither had evidence, but both claimed it. The rabbi suggested that they divide the land or share its use. They rejected the compromise.

The rabbi said, "In that case, I must make a personal visit to the disputed property. Perhaps that will help me reach a decision."

The three went to the property. The rabbi bent down to the ground, mumbled a few words, then set his ear close to the ground. He nodded, then arose and said, "I asked the land to which of you two it belonged. The land said that it belonged to neither. Rather, both of you belong to it, and it will eventually claim both of you.

"Are you not both foolish to argue over something which is so ephemeral? Be wise and accept my compromise to share the land, because it really belongs to neither of you."

From the Scriptures

"If the spirit of a ruler should dwell upon you, do not forsake your place" *(Ecclesiastes 10:4).*

It is clear from the fierce competition in elections that there is something very enticing about holding public office.

It would seem that a true understanding of public office would discourage people from seeking it. R' Gamliel sought to appoint two sages, R' Yochanan and R' Elazar, to public office in order to provide them with a means of livelihood. Being very humble, they refused the honor. R' Gamliel said to them, "Do you think I am giving you a position of authority? I am giving you a position of servitude!" (*Horayos* 10a). Being a "public servant" is hardly a figure of speech. One subjects himself to many masters, and loses his freedom very much as a slave does. Why would anyone desire this?

The only explaination I have is that the drive for recognition must be so overwhelming, it obscures the heavy cost of a position of authority. In *Life's Too Short* I describe a number of maneuvers people use to escape the torment of low self-esteem. I believe that the pursuit of public office to be one of the more desperate of these.

As I have pointed out, good self-esteem and humility go hand-in-hand. Truly humble people have good self esteem, hence they shun positions of authority, e.g., Moses, Saul, and Hillel. They had leadership forced upon them, and accepted it with great reluctance.

There is the danger that power can corrupt. An erstwhile humble person may lose his humility when he assumes a position of authority. Hence, Solomon's wise words: "If the spirit of a ruler should come upon you (if you are thrust into a position of authority), do not forsake your place (do not allow it to rob you of your humility)."

A wise person will shun servitude. If it is forced upon him, he will retain his humility and self-esteem.

From Our Heritage

R' Elchanan Wasserman, the dean of the yeshivah of Baranowitz, was a true disciple of the Chofetz Chaim, and emulated the latter's humility. It is customary for the *chazzan* (reader) not to begin repetition of the *Amidah* until the rabbi has completed the silent prayer. R' Elchanan insisted that the *chazzan* not wait for him, and enforced this practice. One time a newcomer to the yeshivah served as *chazzan*, and being unfamiliar with the practice, waited for R' Elchanan to finish. R' Elchanan said to him sternly, "Are you trying to drive me out of the yeshivah?"

At a gathering in Berlin, the Rebbe of Slonim greeted R' Elchanan by reciting the *berachah* "Blessed is G–d who has shared His wisdom with those who revere Him." R' Elchanan reacted as if he had been bitten by a serpent. He jumped up and seized the rebbe's arm, exclaiming, "No! No!" He was clearly pained when the audience responded by reciting the *berachah* in unison.

"For You listen to the voice of the shofar" *(Rosh Hashanah prayer).*

There are some lengthy prayers on *Rosh Hashanah,* but the most impressive part of the service is the sounding of the shofar. In contrast to all the prayers, the shofar is pure sound without words. If there are no words, what is it that we ask G–d to hear?

Words are limited. There are things we cannot possibly put into words, like the fragrance of a rose. We cannot fully express emotion with words. Sounds are amorphous, and are free of the bounds imposed by words. The infant's cry is more compelling than words.

There are wishes and feelings and expressions of pain that we cannot express in words. The pure sound of the shofar is the vehicle for our communicating these to G–d.

We should understand the limitations of verbal communication. A man came to a rebbe complaining of the strained relations that developed between him and his wife. The rebbe told him to listen carefully to everything she says.

A few days later the man returned. He reported that he was listening faithfully to everything his wife said but that their relationship has not improved. The rebbe said, "Now go home and listen carefully to everything she does *not* say." It takes much greater skill to listen to silence than it does to words.

There are halachic reasons why we do not blow the shofar when *Rosh Hashanah* occurs on Shabbos. There is also a *mussar* concept. On Shabbos we should reach a level of spirituality where we can convey things by silence rather than by sound.

It does not require great wisdom to listen to words. The truly wise person can listen to the communication of silence.

Proper *middos* are a prerequisite for Torah. Without proper *middos,* study of Torah can actually be detrimental. "If a person is meritorious, the Torah becomes an elixir of life. If he is not deserving, the Torah can become a deadly poison" (*Yoma* 72b).

The Maggid of Dubno gave a parable:

A peasant entered a fine clothing store and asked for a suit. The proprietor estimated the man's size, showed him the rack with the size, and told him to choose a suit and put it on in the fitting room.

The peasant soon emerged, cursing the proprietor. "Are you mocking me? This is not my size! It is tight and bulges everywhere!"

The proprietor looked at him and saw that he had put on the suit on top of his thick peasant clothes. "You fool!" he said. "That suit would fit you perfectly. But first you must take off your heavy peasant clothes before you put it on."

We are born with many traits which we must refine. Only then will the Torah "fit us" and be attractive. "Putting on" Torah before we have shed our coarse physical traits can be ugly indeed.

NOTES

_____
_____
_____
_____
_____
_____
_____
_____
_____

Aug. 21, 2004
Sept. 8, 2005

From
the
Sages

"R' Yochanan ben Zakkai asked his disciples, 'Which is the way to which a person should cling?' R' Eliezer said, 'A benevolent eye" (*Ethics of the Fathers 2:13*).

Consciously or unconsciously, we see that which we want to see.

R' Levi Yitzchak of Berditchev once encountered a man who was eating on the fast day of Tishah B'Av. "You have certainly forgotten that today is Tishah B'Av," he said.

"No," the man said. "I know it is Tishah B'Av."

"Ah! Then your doctor forbids you to fast," R' Levi Yitzchak said.

"I am in excellent health," the man answered.

R' Levi Yitzchak lifted his hands toward heaven. "Master of the Universe!" he said. "See how precious Your children are; see this man's love of truth. I gave him several ways to justify his eating on Tishah B'Av, but he would rather incriminate himself than lie. Your nation is so wonderful! Please treat it more mercifully."

Other people might have reacted, "What a defiant scoundrel!" R' Levi Yitzchak had "a benevolent eye." He saw only the good.

A person can become what we think of him. Frankly dishonest people have become honest because someone trusted them.

This is vitally important in parenting. Children may become bad if they sense we think they are bad. In *Positive Parenting* I note that we must learn to discipline children without making them feel bad.

We often catch our children doing something wrong and reprimand them. We must also "catch them" doing things that are right, at least three times a day, and praise them for it.

A wise person will develops his "benevolent eye."

From Our
Heritage

When R' Eliezer fell ill, his disciples visited him. They variously praised his teachings as being superior to the rain, to the sun, and to parents. R' Eliezer did not react. Then R' Akiva spoke up. "Suffering is precious," he said. R' Eliezer then said, "Help me sit so that I can understand what my child Akiva said" (*Sanhedrin* 101a).

Looking back and saying, "See what I have accomplished" is vanity. Looking ahead and saying, "With the skills G–d has given me I hope to accomplish" is self-esteem.

NOTES

R' Eliezer dismissed the comments of his disciples who praised his teachings of the past. Knowing he was terminally ill, he had no hope of teaching again. R' Akiva said, "You are required to do only what you can at any one moment. When you were in good health, your obligation was to teach. Now you cannot do that. But you do have the ability to accept your suffering with faith in G–d. That is now your obligation. Whenever you fulfill your obligation according to the circumstances you are in, that is all that G–d asks of you."

R' Akiva's wise words finally brought comfort to R' Eliezer.

"The transfer of the signet ring (from Ahasuerus to Haman) accomplished what six hundred thousand prophets could not accomplish" *(Eichah Rabbah 4).*

Aug. 22, 2004
Sept. 9, 2005

Six hundred thousand prophets may exert themselves to impress people with the calamity they will bring upon themselves with their errant behavior, but to no avail. Their words fall on deaf ears.

Prophets, spiritual leaders, parents, doctors — all have a shared experience. They warn the populace, their children, or their patients of the consequences of not following instructions, but their words may have no impact. "On deaf ears" is more than a figure of speech. Psychological deafness may be every bit as real as physical deafness. People may be *incapable* of hearing what they do not want to hear. Shouting will not make them hear any better.

I see this phenomenon every day in my practice. Young people are warned about the dangers of drugs. Billions of dollars have been spent on programs to discourage young people from harming themselves. No method has as yet been proven effective.

What shall we do? Stay silent because words are ineffective? No. True, the words of the prophets did not cause people to correct their errant ways. But when Ahasuerus gave Haman the right to do what he wished, the threat of extinction made people hear the message to which they had previously been deaf. We must teach and warn with full knowledge that our words may be ignored. But when improper actions result in imminent danger, what we said will be felt.

There are wise people who will pay heed, and there are wise children who will listen. We can help our children become listeners by learning how to talk to them, and particularly by modeling for them, showing them that *we* listen.

Not far from the home of R' Yeshaye of Prague, a blind man would put up his stand and sell cookies. He often shivered in the cold, and was particularly afraid that the police would fine him for peddling without a permit.

One day, as R' Yeshaye passed by, he saw a policeman confiscate all the blind man's wares. The man wept bitterly. R' Yeshaye asked him how much the cookies were worth, and gave him that amount.

Every day, R' Yeshaye made it his business to pass by the blind man soon after he put up his stand and buy all his cookies. When he was asked why he is doing this, why doesn't he just give the blind man the money, R' Yeshaye answered:

"Don't you understand? This man thinks he is doing me a service by supplying me with cookies. He does not feel that he is accepting charity. He has lost much of the joy of life because he cannot see. Shall I deprive him of this bit of dignity that he can enjoy?"

Our sages knew how to give *tzedakah.*

From Our Heritage

NOTES

Aug. 23, 2004
Sept. 10, 2005

From the Scriptures

"On the second day, the chief of the tribe of Issachar brought his offering..." *(Numbers 7:18).*

This is a most enigmatic Torah portion. There is not a superfluous letter in the Torah. Major *halachos* are derived from a nuance in a sentence or an extra letter. But here the Torah lists the identical offerings of each tribe *twelve times*! Seventy-three verses instead of the single sentence: "Each tribal chief brought this offering!"

There must be an extremely important message here, and Ramban solves the mystery for us. Each tribal chief indeed brought an identical offering, *but not because he imitated his predecessor.* Each chief had made his own calcution in composing his offering. This is the Torah's way of saying, *"Don't imitate. Innovate!"*

A Chassidic rebbe did not do things as his father had. When asked why he did not go in his father's ways, he said, "I *am* following my father's ways. He did not imitate his father; I do not imitate him."

We must clarify: Tradition is vital to *Yiddishkeit*. *Minhagim* (customs) adopted by Jews, whether by all Jews or by one community, are sacred. At times, a *minhag* may override *halachah*. Preserving a *minhag* is not imitating. Emulating *middos* (fine character traits) is not imitating. Doing something just because someone else did it, without thought, that is imitating. We are then doing *his* action, not our own. If we do something we have seen because it is the right thing to do, it is an innovation of our own to do so.

Wise people do not just copy what others do. They learn by carefully studying the actions of others. They think before they do.

From Our Heritage

Heritage need not mean centuries or decades ago. Heritage can mean yesterday, or this morning, if we use what transpired.

When my uncle, the Bobover Rebbe, came to America after the Holocaust, he, relatives, and newcomers lived in a large house in upper Manhattan. The phone arrangement was that each extension had a button which, to assure privacy, cut off all other extensions. The rebbe repeatedly asked, "Before using the button, *please* see if there is a conversation, because you will be cutting people off."

I was sitting in the office when the rebbe was on an important phone call with the president of the fledgling Bobov yeshivah. Abruptly he became silent. Gently, he returned the receiver to its place and said nothing. Then he looked out the window and began humming a melody, drumming with his fingers on the desk.

After some time had passed, he arose and took me by the wrist and said, "Now let us see if we can find who turned the switch while I was talking, and ask him to please not do that again." The offender was talking on the phone. The rebbe waited until he finished his conversation, then gently and softly pointed out to him what had happened, and asked him to please be more considerate.

That is when I learned how to control anger.

NOTES

_____
_____
_____
_____
_____
_____
_____
_____
_____
_____

"Do not forget the teachings of your mother" *(Proverbs 1:8).*

If you think back, you may find that there were things your mother taught you when you were quite young that may have had a greater impact on your life than you thought. Let me share my experiences.

One of the first stories I can remember hearing from my mother, perhaps at age five or six, was that of a poor man who was given one wish. He wished for a purse that would never be empty. He soon found himself in possession of a magic purse which contained a dollar. When he took out the dollar, another dollar appeared in its place. He was overjoyed at having an endless supply of money, and kept on taking out dollars. Several days later he was found dead, lying on a huge pile of dollars.

Did this story of infinite pursuit determine my becoming a specialist in addictive diseases, which are essentially a pursuit of an ever retreating goal? Perhaps.

The other prominent childhood memory is my mother quoting R' Yisrael of Salant, that the problem with the world is that too many people are concerned with the welfare of their own *guf* (body) and other people's *neshamah* (soul). I began my career as a rabbi, occupied with promoting spiritual well being, and changed to becoming a physician, with the prime focus on people's health. Was that my mother's influence? Perhaps.

What does this have to do with wisdom? A wise person will reflect on why he does things. It is important to know one's motivation. Give some thought to Solomon's words. You may be following your mother's teachings.

From Our Heritage

One Chol Hamoed (the intermediate days of Pesach and Succos), R' Isser Zalman Meltzer asked a student for pen and paper. The student was surprised, because he knew that R' Isser Zalman did not write on Chol Hamoed. R' Isser Zalman wrote a few words, and put the slip of paper in his pocket.

Sensing the student's bewilderment, R' Isser Zalman explained, "Many people come to visit me on Chol Hamoed. It's inevitable that among them I will find one or more people who are lacking in full Torah observance. There is the great danger that I will consider myself superior to them.

"I jotted down the verse 'Let your eyes look ahead, but focus toward yourself' *(Proverbs 4:25).* R' Yaakov of Lisa interpreted this to mean that when you see faults in others, find them in yourself. If I become aware in shortcomings of others, I will look at that verse and remind myself that I should be looking at my own.

"Thinking oneself to be superior to others is vanity, a deadly sin. It is permissible to write on Chol Hamoed to save one's health. I needed to write that verse to guard my spiritual health."

Aug. 25, 2004
Sept. 12, 2005

From the Scriptures

"**K**now Him in all your ways, and He will direct your paths aright" *(Proverbs 3:6).*

By now you are aware that I have learned much from my involvement with people recovering from alcohol. I have pointed out that the prophets often refer to errant behavior as a kind of drunkenness, even though alcohol may not be involved. The kinds of things that are conducive to recovery from alcoholism can serve as guidelines to recovery from any improper behavior.

One recovering person cited the statement that sustained recovery requires applying the principles of the recovery program to "*all* one's affairs." He went on to say, "If you are not spiritual in all your affairs, then you are spiritual in none." This did not sit well with me. I believe that each *mitzvah* a person does is of value, even if he may be derelict in keeping others.

Yet what this man said reminded me of the above verse in *Proverbs.* The condition that will merit G–d guiding you in the right direction is for you to know Him in *all* your ways.

I believe this apparent conflict can be resolved. We may be derelict in not doing what we should, but our goal should be to *become* whole. We should aim to improve in those areas where we are deficient. The Talmud states that a sincere intent in doing a *mitzvah* is considered a *mitzvah.* If we have not reached the point where we "know G–d in everything we do," we should be trying to get there. If, however, we divide our lives, believing that we should observe Torah only in areas that pertain to religious ritual but that Torah does not apply to our daily life activities, then even our ritual observance is suspect.

Wise people know that spirituality is not confined to ritual. We must try to become spiritual in everything we do.

From Our Heritage

NOTES

My father used to quote the verse, "You shall not revile G–d" (*Exodus* 22:27) and cite the commentary who said that the Hebrew words can also be interpreted as, "One who is G–dly does not revile anyone." He would tell me that when my grandmother became angry at someone, she would say, "May he have fresh, soft bread and cold, hard butter." That was the worst curse she could utter.

Before the Six Day War, when Nasser of Egypt appeared to pose a threat to the existence of Israel, someone told R' Aryeh Levin to curse Nasser and eliminate him from the world scene. R' Aryeh responded, "I don't know how to curse. I can bless Nasser that he should live to see the speedy coming of Moshiach. Then he will be unable to make us any *tzaros.*"

"A word is worth one *selah*; silence is worth two" *(Megillah 18a).*

Aug. 26, 2004
Sept. 13, 2005

I have already discussed the value of silence and the problems that can arise from improper speech. However, I came across an aphorism which rephrases this Talmudic statement, and I wish to add to this theme. The aphorism is, "Wisdom is the reward you get for listening when you'd rather be talking." A corollary aphorism is, "Wisdom never enters the brain through the mouth."

As these highlight, unwise speech is harmful, but another reason to be silent is that *while you're talking, you can't be listening.*

We often think that what we have to say is incredibly wise. Only afterwards may we realize that it was not that wise after all. It is much like the bright ideas we have in a dream. If we wake up and jot them down and then look at them in the morning, we may be shocked to see that they were simply gibberish. Much the same can happen during waking hours. And while we were talking, we could not possibly listen. In fact, with our talk we may have silenced someone who did have something of substance to say.

Note that the Talmud is not comparing silence to worthless speech, but to speech that is worth a *selah*. Even then, silence is worth two. Under the best of circumstances, when what we have to say is in fact wise, it may contribute to other people's wisdom, but it adds nothing to our own. We already know what it is we are going to say. If we keep silent, we lose nothing of our own wisdom and there is a fair chance that we may gain something.

If we had the opportunity to make an investment where there is no risk of any loss and a fair chance of gain, would we not invest? The wise person will apply the same principle to speech.

From Our Heritage

My grandfather, the rebbe of Bobov, lived in Tchebin for a period of time. He once participated in a *sheva berachos* (post-wedding celebration) at which R' Dov Weidenfeld, the Rav of Tchebin, was present. The discussion turned to whether the *Lechaim* was to be provided by the bride's or the groom's family. My grandfather said, "It appears from *Tosafos* (a commentary on the Talmud) that it is the groom's responsibility." R' Dov, who had the entire Talmud at his fingertips, remarked, "There is no such *Tosafos*."

Several years later, R' Dov was giving a Talmudic lecture to yeshivah students when he abruptly paused and said, "This *Tosafos* does indeed indicate that it is the groom's responsibility! The Bobover Rebbe was right."

R' Dov then explained to the class the discussion of several years earlier. "When I said that there was no such *Tosafos*, the Bobover Rebbe could have quoted this *Tosafos* and shown me that I was wrong. Yet he said nothing, to avoid putting me to shame. To restrain oneself from demonstrating that one was right in order to protect another person's honor is one of the most difficult things to do."

ELUL

אלול

Aug. 27, 2004
Sept. 14, 2005

From Our Prayers

"Blessed are You, King of the universe, Who gave the rooster understanding to distinguish between day and night" *(Morning prayers).*

This does appear to be a rather strange blessing. Some commentaries explain that the Hebrew word for "rooster" can also mean "heart." But how does the heart distinguish between day and night?

Let us stay with the original meaning. There is significance in the rooster's crowing at dawn.

Just when is dawn? If we could establish with precision the astronomical moment when night ends and day begins, we would find that the conditions before and after the moment of dawn are essentially indistinguishable. It is just as dark a minute after dawn as it was a minute before dawn. Our vision cannot discern the difference. Left to our own devices, we might say it is night when it is in fact day and vice versa. The rooster has a sense perception that is sensitive to this imperceptible change.

What does this tell us? That there are subtle changes that are as distinct as that of day and night, but we may not be able to distinguish them. Anyone can tell the difference between midday and midnight, but the difference between day and night at dawn is much more difficult to discern.

Anyone can tell that crime is wrong and charity is right. But there are gray areas where the difference between right and wrong is much less blatant. We may make an ethical or moral judgment that is wrong, but it may seem right to us. Our intelligence is not as acute in distinguishing right from wrong as the rooster's instinct is to distinguish day from night.

In absence of such an instinct, we would be wise to seek advice from wise people on ethical and moral issues. Even though the differences may be subtle, right and wrong are as opposite as day and night.

From Our Heritage

NOTES

Have you ever found out someone's direct phone line or private number and taken advantage of it?

R' Yaakov Kamnetzky's wife was to undergo surgery, and he wished to obtain a *berachah* from R' Moshe Feinstein. He called R' Moshe, but as so often happened, the line was constantly busy.

Someone said to R' Yaakov, "You have the number of R' Moshe's private line. You can easily reach him that way."

R' Yaakov responded, "That number was given to me when I had to reach R' Moshe for a decision that affected the *klal* (the community). My call now is for a personal matter. I don't have the right to use his private number for that."

"**E**very man has three characters— that which he exhibits, that which he has, and that which he thinks he has."

Words of Wisdom

ELUL

11

אלול

Aug. 28, 2004
Sept. 15, 2005

I believe that whatever is true in psychology can be found in Torah. The above psychological observation is stated in Midrash. "A person is called by three names: that given to him by his parents, that which others call him, and that which he calls himself" (*Tanchuma Vayakhel* 8). "That which he has" is the character he was endowed with at birth, which his parents gave him. "That which he exhibits" is the one that others call him. And "that which he thinks he has" is the one he calls himself.

The purpose of the Midrash telling us this is that having three names, i.e., three personalities, is confusing. It means that a person must function in three different ways, and this can drain one's energy. I suspect that our great Torah personalities were able to achieve so much in spiritual growth because they had resolved this tripartite composition that most people struggle with. They only had to be one person, to G–d, to others, and to themselves.

We are born with a number of traits. These can be channeled in good or bad directions. The Midrash states that Moses was born with traits that could have been very obnoxious, but that he transformed them into excellent traits (*Tiferes Yisrael*, end of *Kiddushin*). Moses had nothing to hide from others, and had no need to defend his character. It had become pure and noble. The self that he knew he had was the one that he exhibited to others. There was no dissimulation. Our great Torah personalities followed in the footsteps of Moses.

Moses is referred to as *Rabbeinu*, our teacher. His teachings are not only the word of G–d which he conveyed to us, but the way he lived, and particularly, the transformation of his character traits. If we wish to be wise, we will learn from our great teacher. We do not have to be fragmented. We can be one character, and all three names can be blended to form one name.

From Our Heritage

NOTES

If we wish to be considerate, we must think ahead. What will be the consequences of my actions?

Before *Succos*, the Steipler Gaon went into a store to buy a *lulav* (palm branch). After examining all of them, he find none of which he approved. He then chose one at random, paid for it, and left.

Someone who had observed him asked, "I do not understand. You were obviously not satisfied with any of the *lulavim*. Why did you buy this one?"

The Steipler answered, "Oh, I don't plan to use it. But if I had left the store without a *lulav*, word might spread that no *lulavim* in this store are kosher. They are kosher, but I was looking for a special *lulav*. Why should I cast aspersions on this store's merchandise?"

Aug. 29, 2004
Sept. 16, 2005

From the Sages

"**There are three crowns: the crown of Torah, the crown of priesthood, and the crown of kingdom. But the crown of a good name is superior to all**" *(Ethics of the Fathers 4:17).*

It has been said, "The good things of life last a number of days, but a good name, for days without number."

Priesthood and kingdom are not within everyone's reach. If one was not born a *kohen* one cannot become a *kohen*. If one is not in the line of royalty, the chances of becoming a king are very slim. Although Torah is within everyone's reach, there are some people who were not given a Torah education, and although they may learn Torah, they are unlikely to become outstanding scholars. But everyone can acquire a good name. It is its accessibility that makes it superior to the other three.

Some people attach their names to objects, such as buildings and monuments. These tell us nothing commendable about the person. We can visit the triumphant Arch of Titus in the ruins of the Roman forum. Who thinks well of Titus?

A good name can be preserved in family tradition. People who have helped support synagogues and yeshivos may have their names perpetuated in these structures. This tells us that these people valued Torah and *Yiddishkeit. Sefarim* (Torah books) that bear a donor's name tell us the person valued Torah and wished to make it more accessible to others. Even if a person's circumstances were such that he did not have a knowledge of Torah, his good name is perpetuated in the Torah he helped make available to others.

The founder of Chassidus is refered to as the Baal Shem Tov. A wise person realizes that everyone can live a life that will make him a "Baal Shem Tov," the owner of a good name.

From Our Heritage

R' Dovid of Lelov said, "How can you think of me as a *tzaddik*, when I feel greater love for my own child than for another's child?"

R' Dovid had a son who was beloved by the community. One time the child became seriously ill and the doctors gave up hope. People assembled in the synagogues to pray for him and gave *tzedakah* to merit his recovery. When the child recovered, the townsfolk came to R' Dovid to celebrate the glad tidings. To their surprise, they found R' Dovid in tears.

"Why are you crying?" they asked. "We are all so happy that G-d accepted our prayers for your son."

R' Dovid replied, "Yes, for my child people gathered in the synagogues and prayed fervently. They gave *tzedakah* for his welfare, and their prayers were answered. But what happens to other sick children? No one knows about them. No one cares about them. No one prays for them. It is for them that I am crying."

NOTES

"When a person's ways please G–d, He shall make even his enemies be at peace with him" *(Proverbs 16:7).*

Aug. 30, 2004
Sept. 17, 2005

In *Path of the Just* R' Moshe Chaim Luzzato says that there is nothing as sweet as revenge. The Torah's restriction against revenge can be a most difficult challenge with which to cope. Solomon takes this further. If misfortune befalls your enemy, you may feel he received his just desserts, and you may wish to celebrate. You may feel that G–d did to him what you were not permitted to. Solomon warns, "When your enemy falls, do not rejoice, and when he stumbles, do not let your heart be glad. Lest G–d see it and it displease Him, and He takes away His anger from him" (*Proverbs* 24:17-18).

Solomon's reasoning is that G–d may have reason for punishing your enemy, but it has nothing to do with you. It is a private account. If you take undeserved credit for his punishment, G–d may stop it. You may actually be undoing what you wanted to do.

There is another reason not to rejoice at an enemy's misery. We should feel a kinship with other people, even an enemy. Rejoicing at another's suffering rejects the bond that should unite all humans.

We are to emulate G–d. The Midrash states that when the Egyptians were drowned in the Red Sea, the heavenly angels wished to sing praises to G–d for His judgment. G–d silenced them saying, "The works of My hands are drowning, and you wish to sing My praises?" Although the Divine judgement was that they be punished, G–d was not happy that He had to make that judgment.

Solomon suggests, "If your enemy is hungry, give him bread to eat; if he is thirsty, give him water to drink. You will be heaping coals on his head" (*Proverbs* 25:21-22). Retaliation will give him more reason to act against you. Be kind to him, and you will disarm him.

Wise people will deal with their enemies in a way that is more likely to stop their hostile behavior.

R' Yosef Kahaneman, rav and *rosh yeshivah* of Ponevezh, solicited a wealthy man in support of the yeshivah. The man, who was totally assimilated, gave a generous contribution and then said:

"I abandoned *Yiddishkeit* many years ago. I mingled with Gentile friends, and they urged me to convert. I thought this would help me socially and in business. Only one thing held me back.

"When I was a young boy, I went to Radin to learn. There was no place for me to stay, and the Chofetz Chaim took me into his home. He gave me a place to sleep. I was half asleep when I felt someone near me. It was the Chofetz Chaim, who was covering me with his kaftan. I later saw him sitting at the table learning in his shirtsleeves. The kaftan that he usually wore was my cover.

"I know I am not the *Yid* I should be, but the warmth of that kaftan has kept me a *Yid*."

From Our Heritage

NOTES

Aug. 31, 2004
Sept. 18, 2005

From the Sages

"Just as it is a *mitzvah* to say things that will be heard, so it is a *mitzvah* to refrain from saying things that will not be heard" *(Yevamos 68b).*

One is obligated to give guidance, even rebuke, to those acting improperly. One who fails to do so bears responsibilty for the wrongs. In this passage the Talmud qualifies this. In certain cases, one must offer constructive criticism only when it may be accepted. If he knows his words will fall on deaf ears, he should be silent.

The reason the Talmud gives is that if the transgressor is not aware that what he is doing is wrong, he is only an inadvertent transgressor. If he is told his actions are wrong and persists in them, he is an intentional transgressor and his sin is greater. If you know the person will not cease his errant behavior, it may be better to let him be an inadvertent transgressor. Do not increase his culpability.

There is another reason, one particularly important in parenting. By giving a child an order you know he will disobey, you undermine your authority. Once a child disobeys a parent, it is easier for him to be disobedient again.

Parents should be adroit. If they know a child will disobey an explicit order, they should let him know how they feel about the issue. Hopefully, the parent-child relationship will keep the child from doing something of which the parents disapprove.

It is important that parents explain to the child the reason for their position. If the child still goes against their wishes, the parents may express their disappointment. If the child's disobedience results in undesirable consequences, this is not the time for a triumphant "I told you so." Rather, parents should rationally point out to the child why it is to his advantage to heed their advice.

Wise parents and wise people will give careful consideration to what they instruct others and how they criticize. Let us not undermine our own effectiveness.

From Our Heritage

NOTES

_____
_____
_____
_____
_____
_____
_____

The Torah states several times, "You shall love the newcomer to Israel" (e.g., *Deuteronomy* 10:19).

One *Simchas Torah,* a convert to Judaism met the Chazon Ish on his return from shul, and tearfully complained that people show him no respect at all. "What happened to the *mitzvah* to love the newcomer to Judaism?" he asked.

The Chazon Ish tried to comfort him, and then said, "Perhaps you know a *Simchas Torah* tune to dance?" The man did not hesitate, and began singing a merry melody aloud. The Chazon Ish took him by the hands and danced with him in the street for all passersby to see, until he felt that the man's anguish had been relieved.

"I believe with complete faith that there will be resuscitation of the dead whenever the will emanates from the Creator"** *(Thirteen Principles of Faith).*

"G–d will resurrect the dead," said R' Mendel of Kotzk. "I wish to resurrect the living."

Why do the living need to be resurrected? The rebbe of Kotzk was extremely insightful. His comment parallels that of a wise man who was asked whether he believed there is life after death. He answered, "A more important question is, 'Is there life after birth?' "

On 18 Tammuz we noted the Talmudic saying that "The wicked are considered dead even when they live" (*Berachos* 18a). We noted that physiologic life is essentially animal in nature. Animals, too, eat, sleep, and move around. The uniqueness of humans is that they can be spiritual. If people fail to be spiritual, their animal component is alive, but their human component is lifeless.

Spirituality can be very demanding. It requires that we suppress many of our physiological drives. It requires that we give up our comfort in order to do things for others. Spirituality requires that we set an ultimate goal in life other than just being content and maximizing our pleasure. Spirituality conceives that there can be happiness even when one suffers. Spirituality requires much effort, but the natural response of our bodies is inertia, hence the natural response to spirituality is one of resistance.

The dead will not offer resistance to resurrection. It is the living whose spirit is lifeless that may resist being resurrected. The miracle of resurrecting the live may be greater than resurrecting the dead.

Wise people will wish to be fully alive. They will assist and participate in efforts to enliven their spirit.

The Talmud says that while most people are not immoral, the majority of people are guilty of *gezeilah* (taking other people's money. *Bava Basra* 165a). But we are all honest people. We would never take a person's money or belongings. Why does the Talmud accuse us all of *gezeilah*?

When R' Isser Zalman Meltzer was invited to a wedding or other celebration, he would stand outdoors awaiting the taxi. Sometimes this wait was prolonged.

"Why do you have to wait outdoors?" he was asked. "Remain inside and the taxi driver will blow the horn when he arrives."

R' Isser Zalman said, "The people who are sending the taxi for me are paying for it. If the driver has to wait for me, there will be an additional charge to them. What right do I have to cause these people a monetary loss?"

Let us reflect. Are we really cautious not to cause others a monetary loss?

From Our Heritage

NOTES

From the Scriptures

"**Have you shown weakness on the day of adversity? Then your real adversity was your lack of strength**" *(Proverbs 24:10).*

A man complained to the rebbe about his many *tzaros* (distresses). The rebbe told him to pray and G-d will help him. "But I don't know how to pray properly," the man said.

"Then *that* is your real *tzarah*," the rebbe replied.

Life has many adversities. Some people seem to be better able to cope with and survive very difficult challenges, while other people are crushed by stresses of lesser intensity.

The verse states, "Man was created to struggle" *(Job* 2:7). The sages teach, "G-d does not give a person a burden he cannot carry" *(Shemos Rabbah* 34:1). The two balance: We all face challenges in life, but none of them are beyond our capacity to cope.

I often make reference to the problem of low self-esteem. Many people are unaware of their strengths. I believe that is the work of the *yetzer hara*, who seeks to cripple and disable the person. We must resist the *yetzer hara's* cunning. We must know that G-d gives us the wherewithal to cope with the challenges He poses for us.

It is easier to blame our difficulties on external problems rather than on our own shortcomings. We then seek to fix "things" rather than ourselves. How often do people think that if they change jobs, locales, or marriage partners, their problems will be resolved? Changing external circumstances leaves the self unchanged, and manipulating the environment rarely results in lasting relief.

Solomon was right, and wise people will heed his words. The greatest adversity is not outside of us, but in our failure to fully develop our inner strengths.

From Our Heritage

NOTES

On Judgment Day we will be asked, "Did you treat our fellow man with proper dignity?'

There was an elderly man who would say the assigned *Ma'amodos* (ancillary prayers) each day of the week. One day he did not have the time to finish them. The following day he came to R' Aharon Kotler, asking whether it is permissible for him to finish today the *Ma'amodos* that he omitted yesterday.

It was hardly a difficult question. Clearly, one may say these prayers any day. But to dismiss the question simply would be insulting. The man may think that his prayers were of little substance.

R' Aharon took a volume of the Jerusalem Talmud and studied it, probably in preparation for a *shiur* (lecture). After about ten minutes he said to the man, "You may say yesterday's *Ma'amodos* today."

R' Aharon had not wasted a minute. He also made the person feel that his question was important enough to warrant serious consideration.

"He who sends a message by the hand of a fool cuts off his own feet and will taste distortion" *(Proverbs 26:6).*

From the Scriptures

ELUL

17

אלול

Sept. 3, 2004
Sept. 21, 2005

A person must delegate. If one tries to do everything himself, he may be too overwhelmed to accomplish all he must. However, he must be careful whom he selects to represent and assist him.

The Talmud states, "An agent is like the principal" (*Berachos* 34b). Though this means that the actions of an agent have the same status as those of the principal, we should also take it to mean that people assume that the agent is carrying out the will of the principal. It is therefore essential that one choose a trustworthy person to accurately convey his position.

We previously noted the disaster that befell our people because a messenger erred. An error in the messenger's misunderstanding of the message can result in the recipient giving a wrong reply, and this may set in motion a chain of events with unfortunate results.

The Talmud says, "Scholars, be cautious with your words. They may be distorted and cause a calamity" (*Ethics of the Fathers* 1:11). We can exercise caution with our own words, but when we put them in the hands of an emissary, we have no guarantee that they will be faithfully conveyed.

If you are interviewed by a reporter, particularly on a sensitive subject, ask to have your quote read back to you. You may be surprised at what you hear. By the same token, if you read something that another person said that displeases you, do not be hasty to criticize. He may not have said what was written.

Wise people will watch their own words and will be doubly cautious when they let someone speak for them.

From Our Heritage

Torah observance requires meticulous attention to the *Shulchan Aruch* (Code of Law). Some want to be more stringent than the law requires. While commendable, this requires consistency. This anecdote shows how it may be wrong to go beyond the requirment.

When the scholar, R' Yehoshua Leib Diskin, was a child, his father, R' Binyamin, allowed the boy to eat things that he himself did not eat. The young Yehoshua Leib once asked his father, "If this is kosher, why do you not eat it? If it is not, why may I eat it?"

R' Binyamin answered, "It is certainly kosher. Why I abstain is something you will one day understand."

"Years later," R' Yehoshua Leib continued, "a man came to tell my father that a shul had burned and its Torah scrolls were destroyed. I led him in, and as soon as my father heard of the destruction of the scrolls, he fainted, and was revived with great difficulty.

"I then understood. If I did not react this way when I heard of the destruction of the Torah scrolls, I was clearly not at my father's spiritual level. It was appropriate for him to take upon himself more than the law required, but not for me."

NOTES

From the Sages

"A person should pray that he retain his faculties in his old age" *(Tanchumah Miketz).*

Of course one should pray to have good physical and mental health in old age. However, we have a principle that "Prayer achieves half" *(Vayikra Rabbah* 10:5). We must provide for the other half ourselves.

We should do whatever is necessary to preserve our health and avoid the things that may damage us; e.g., smoking, excessive drinking, overeating. People are generally aware of the importance of physical fitness.

Unfortunately, not much attention is given to psychological fitness. In the working years people may think that there is nothing better than having all the leisure time one wants. When retirement brings unlimited leisure time, many people do not know what to do with themselves.

Some people look forward to the retirement years because they will have the time to play golf, go fishing, and do all the things they had no time for previously. In the event that the wear and tear diseases of advanced years preclude physical activity, they may be sorely disillusioned.

Torah scholars welcome leisure time. It gives them the opportunity to pursue Torah studies that they could not attend to during their working years. Perhaps this is what the psalmist meant, "They will still be fruitful in their old age; vigorous and fresh will they be" *(Psalms* 92:15).

Many people plan for financial security in their old age. Wise people also plan for their psychological and spiritual well being.

From Our Heritage

R' Naftali Tzvi Berlin (the *Netziv*) and R' Yitzchak Elchanan traveled to St. Petersburg to appeal that the government remove some edicts directed against the Jews. This vital cause required them to remain there over *Rosh Hashanah.* They went to the shul of the "Cantonists," men who had, as youths, been forcefully taken from their homes and inducted to the Czar's army for twenty-five years.

One of these soldiers delivered a "sermon" before the services. "My brothers," he said. "Today Jews throughout the world pray to G–d for long life, livelihood, and *nachas* from their children. For what can we pray? We must always be ready to give up our lives for the Czar. We may not marry and have children. All our needs are provided for by the Czar. We have nothing personal to ask of G–d. There is only one thing we can pray for. Join me, my brothers, to pray that G–d reveal His sovereignty and glory to the entire world, and that all peoples of the world recognize Him as the true G–d."

The *Netziv* and R' Yitzchak Elchanan wept at this expression of sincere devotion to G–d.

NOTES

_____
_____
_____
_____
_____
_____
_____
_____

"For the fate of man and the fate of the beast—they have one and the same fate...Man has no superiority over beast, for all is futile" *(Ecclesiastes 3:19).*

From the Scriptures

Sept. 5, 2004
Sept. 23, 2005

This thought is not only discouraging and depressing, but also contradicts everything we believe about the greatness of man. This verse is contained in the morning prayers, but with the addendum that we, as children of Abraham, Isaac, and Jacob, are redeemed in being able to serve G–d. Solomon does not provide this qualification. What can his words mean?

R' Mendel of Kotzk translated the above verse a bit differently. "The superiority of man over beast is *ayin* (nothing) ; i.e., man has the capacity to efface himself before G–d and know that he is nothing. Animals lack this capacity."

The greatness of man lies in his humility. Animals do not self-efface. They are totally preoccupied with self-gratification. They exist only for themselves.

R' Mendel points out that a seed that is planted in the ground must disintegrate before it can produce a plant. Man is no different. He must shed all sense of self to be productive.

R' Mendel is careful to point out that such self-effacement does not mean low self-worth. Humility actually precludes self-deprecation. "A person must say, 'The world was created for me'" (*Sanhedrin* 37a). A human being should have enormous self-worth in the knowledge that he was created to fulfill a Divine mission.

The person who indulges in physical gratification lowers himself to the animal level. He does not see himself as *ayin.* The person who pursues spiritual growth and effaces the physically driven ego is superior to the beast.

Wisdom and humility go together. The wise take pride in their human uniqueness, but are humble.

From Our Heritage

NOTES

Two yeshivah students came to R' Dov Weidenfeld of Tchebin to inform him that the administrator of an institution that cares for the poor was seriously ill. They gave the rabbi his name and asked for his *berachah* (blessing) for recovery.

A while after the two left R' Dov abruptly said, "Oy! How foolish of me! I did not understand!"

The student who attended R' Dov asked, "What is the problem?"

"Do you think they came for my *berachah*? Me? My *berachah* has special value? It was just a polite way to tell me that the administrator's illness caused the institution not to have enough money to provide for the poor. I just did not understand." The student's insistence that they really came for a *berachah* fell on deaf ears.

R' Dov took out a sum of money, and did not rest until the money was delivered to the institution.

From the Scriptures

"**The hand of the diligent will reach mastery, while negligent laxity (remiyah) will cause dependence**" *(Proverbs 12:24)*.

One of the repetitive themes in *Proverbs* is the ruinous trait of indolence. Time after time, Solomon condemns sloth and laziness. What is of interest, however, is that in contrasting indolence with industriousness, Solomon often uses the Hebrew word *remiyah*, which generally means "deceit" or "trickery," as meaning "indolence." This use of *remiyah* is not haphazard.

A diligent person is conscious of his purpose on earth and dedicates himself to fulfilling that purpose. Judaism asserts that the purpose of man's existence is achieved by observance of the Torah. Inasmuch as one cannot carry out the dictates of the Torah unless one is in good health and can function, anything that is conducive to optimal health becomes part of Torah observance. Eating, sleeping, and earning a livelihood can therefore be considered Torah observance when one engages in them for that purpose.

Rest and relaxation are also essential for optimal health. How much? Here we are on unsure grounds. We know approximately how many calories a person requires, and we may assume that the average person requires between six to eight hours of sleep. But how much relaxation is enough?

A person might rationalize that he needs a great deal of relaxation and diversion, and indulge in these far more than is necessary for his health. He will convince himself that he is not lazy, but this is what his body and mind need. He is deceiving himself by rationalizing his indolence. This is how indolence is *remiyah*, deceit.

It is morally wrong to deceive others. It is utter folly to deceive oneself. Wise people will not commit the folly of self-deceit.

From Our Heritage

NOTES

The history of bitter anti-Semitism in Europe is all too familiar.

The senior health official in Altona, Germany, said that the Jewish cemetery was a swamp that was a breeding ground for danergous insects, and he wanted the cemetery to be covered with cement.

R' Yaakov Etlinger (author of *Aruch LaNer*) pleaded with the mayor to revoke the order. The mayor agreed to send a scientist to study the cemetery, which had moist earth, but was hardly a swamp.

On the day the scientist was to examine the cemetery, the Jewish population of Altona fasted. R' Yaakov and ten Torah scholars prayed at the gravesides of the *tzaddikim* who were buried there. As they wept, their tears fell upon *parched earth*. Suddenly the cemetery appeared as if after a severe drought. When the investigator came, he could not but report that the land was unusually dry and could not support any insect breeding.

The prayers of the populace had produced a miracle.

"**F**ortunate is the generation in which the greater listen to the lesser" *(Rosh Hashanah 25b).*

From the Sages

ELUL

21

אלול

Sept. 7, 2004
Sept. 25, 2005

This would seem to contradict the Talmudic statement dicussed previously that listening to the counsel of the young can be destructive. In fact, however, there is no conflict. We should consider the advice of everyone, old or young, great or small. When the Talmud says that a wise person is one who learns from everyone (*Ethics of the Fathers* 4:1), it means from the younger and lesser as well. The words of the elders should be considered more authoritative, but the ideas of youth should not be dismissed.

When I was a fledgling psychiatric resident, I referred a patient to one of the foremost, internationally acknowledged psychiatrists. I was flabbergasted when I received a call from this psychiatrist, who wished to discuss this case with me. I explained to him that I was just a beginner and knew little about treatment. He said, "Yes, I may know more about treatment, but you know more about this person." When I told my instructor that I was consulted by this world famous psychiatrist, he said, "The only one who would do that is the one who wrote the authoritative book on the subject. He does not have to protect his ego."

Some doctors may feel insulted when the patient asks them to call in a consultant. They may agree only to a consultant who is chief of the department at the hospital or medical school. Consulting anyone of lesser stature is an affront to their ego. People with good self-esteem and a healthy ego do not feel threatened by taking advice from anyone.

The Talmud says, "Wherever you find the greatness of G–d, there you find His humility" (*Megillah* 31a). Contrary to what one may think, the greatness of a person is shown not by how much he knows, but by how much he is willing to learn.

Young people may have fresh ideas that may be very valuable. We would be wise to listen to them.

From Our Heritage

One of the Chofetz Chaim's young grandchildren asked him, "Zeide, how old are you?" The Chofetz Chaim embraced the child, smiled, but did not answer his question.

After a bit, the Chofetz Chaim put a few bills into an envelope and gave it to the grandchild. "Here is gift for you," he said.

The child thanked him and put the envelope in his pocket. "Aren't you curious how much is inside?" the Chofetz Chaim asked.

"I appreciate whatever Zeide gave me," the child said. "It's not polite to count the money in the presence of the giver."

"So it is with me," the Chofetz Chaim said. "Every day, every moment of life is a gift from G–d. Do we really appreciate the value of every moment of life? It is not polite to count a gift, is it?"

NOTES

_____
_____
_____
_____
_____
_____

Sept. 8, 2004
Sept. 26, 2005

From the Sages

"**A**t the head of the list of thieves are those who steal the minds of others" *(Tosefta Bava Kamma 7).*

The expression "stealing the minds of others" to refer to a person who deceives or dissimulates is an interesting idiom. Our sages chose their words wisely.

If a person believes you, he gives you his trust. If you are truthful, you return that trust. If you are untruthful, you have taken his trust and returned nothing. This is a form of theft. Our sages place this at the top of the list, for they see it as a forerunner to other theft.

This insight of our sages is profound. We may not consciously consider dissimulating as being theft, but that is how it registers in our subconscious minds, and the effects can be far reaching. Once you commit theft of any kind, your resistance to and abhorrence of theft is compromised, and this can lead to frank thievery.

But of even greater importance is the effect it can have on our children. Inasmuch as dissimulation is perceived subconsciously as a kind of theft, it may set a dangerous precedent for children. Parents who are shocked to discover that their child has been dishonest or has stolen should examine themselves to see whether they have ever presented themselves to other people as anything other than they are. Parents who consider themselves scrupulously honest in that they have never misappropriated even a cent of other people's money should realize that if they dissimulated, they were actually modeling for their children that thievery is permissible.

The Talmud says that not only the teachings but even the conversation of our sages should be carefully studied *(Succah* 21b). What may seem to be an idiom is a profound psychological insight and an important guideline in parenting

From Our Heritage

NOTES

_____
_____
_____
_____
_____
_____
_____
_____

R' Yisrael of Salant was giving a public lecture on a complicated Talmudic topic in Vilna. A scholar in the audience challenged a point he made. R' Yisrael paused and descended from the pulpit. He was overheard saying to himself, "Yisrael, don't you learn *mussar?*" He later explained that he had five refutations to the challenge, but because he did not feel that any of them was completely valid, he admitted that the scholar's challenge was correct.

R' Eliyahu Lopian explained R' Yisrael's pause before alighting. The purpose in his lecture was not to show his erudition in Talmud. Rather, because of the opposition to the study of *mussar,* which R' Yisrael promoted, he felt that if people were impressed with his Talmudic knowledge, they would acknowledge his authority and accept *mussar.* He considered rebutting the challenge to promote *mussar.* However, he concluded that since the rebuttals were not fully valid, a triumph for *mussar* in a way inconsistent with *mussar* was unacceptable. These were his thoughts during the brief pause.

"For oppression makes the wise foolish, and a gift corrupts the heart" *(Ecclesiastes 7:7).*

Sept. 9, 2004
Sept. 27, 2005

This is generally understood to mean that the judgment of the wise can be distorted by both duress and bribery. Rashi gives another interpretation, based on the Midrash: "The provocation of a fool can disarm the wise person and can destroy his understanding." As an example, he cites the case of Moses, who was provoked by Dathan and Aviram following his initial meeting with Pharoah. They accused Moses of worsening the plight of the Israelites, causing Moses to complain to G–d. This reaction contributed to the decree that Moses would not enter the Promised Land.

We are often subject to provocation. People are sometimes accused unjustly. The anger this arouses may cause the person to respond without his applying his usual good judgment.

A *tzaddik* was once attacked in the street by a woman who mistook him for the husband who had abandoned her. She realized her mistake and apologized profusely. The *tzaddik* said, "You did not intend to attack me personally. I was not at all offended. And as for the blows I received, Heaven knows I probably deserved them."

Provocation may cause us to feel guilty for doing something. The natural tendency is to defend ourselves by counterattacking. But this may compound our problem. If we remember that provocation can make us respond foolishly, we may be able to restrain ourselves. Then we will have no need to regret our response.

Wise people will take great precaution to avoid acting foolishly.

From Our Heritage

Bribery does not always manifest itself in gifts or in favors. We may sometimes be "bribed" by wishing to accommodate to public opinion.

R' Yosef Dov of Brisk once fell seriously ill, and his son R' Chaim was summoned. When R' Chaim arrived, he heard the people say that his father's condition was critical, and that he was not expected to live for more than a few hours. When he entered the sick room, the doctor told him that his father's condition was hopeless.

R' Chaim promptly brought in another physician who prescribed a treatment which was effective. R' Chaim explained, "When I heard that the attending doctor's opinion was similar to that of the people, I suspected that his judgment might have been affected by their attitude of despair. I felt that another doctor who was free of this pessimistic attitude might think of a treatment that had escaped the other doctor."

R' Chaim's son, R' Velvele, said that he applied his father's teaching to evaluating even halachic opinions. "When a *posek* (halachic authority) gives a ruling that is in conformity with the public's wishes, it deserves greater scrutiny."

NOTES

Sept. 10, 2004
Sept. 28, 2005

From the Scriptures

"**B**laze a trail, clear a path, remove the obstacles from the way of my people"** *(Isaiah 57:14).*

"**A** voice calls out in the wilderness, 'Clear a path for return to G–d. Make a straight road in the plain, a road to our G–d' "** *(Isaiah 40:3).*

The message is that the path to G–d is full of obstacles. They must be removed. This requires work. Reaching G–d is not easy.

It has been correctly said that "If you find a path with no obstacles, it probably does not lead anywhere."

Torah thinkers teach that before a *neshamah* comes to this world, it is in G–d's Presence, basking in His glory. But this is a delight which the *neshamah* did not earn. The Zohar refers to it as "bread of humiliation," like the feeling of a pauper who begs for food. His hunger is relieved, but it costs him the humiliation of begging. His food is garnished with suffering. Similarly, the *neshamah* can truly enjoy the delight of the Divine glory by earning it.

We often look for easy ways to do things. Technology has given us conveniences we can activate with the touch of a button.

Preparing kosher chicken used to be a process. The chicken had to be opened, soaked, and salted. Now we buy pre-koshered chicken. Packaged foods have eliminated much preparation.

We might think that all Torah observance should be with similar ease. However, our mission is to *earn* the delight for the *neshamah.* We must make our way to G–d by overcoming the hurdles and eliminating the obstacles placed by the *yetzer hara.* The aphorism is true. If we have no obstacles, we are likely not on the right path.

From Our Heritage

NOTES

It is not unusual to find people arguing in shul, sometimes with rancor, for the privilege of leading the services. Each is observing a *yahrzeit* (memorial for a departed parent), and each wishes to honor the parent's memory by leading the service.

R' Eliyahu Dessler (author of *Michtav M'Eliyahu)* forewent visiting his father's grave because he believed that teaching Torah was a greater merit than visiting the grave. However, on the eve of the *yahrzeit,* he abruptly left Gateshead for London, even though this precluded his saying *kaddish* at the evening service.

R' Dessler explained his action. "I received a call from London that a *shidduch* (proposed marriage) was in imminent danger of being dissolved. Although I am an only son and there is no one else to say *kaddish* for my father, I felt it was a greater merit for him that I rescue an appropriate *shidduch* than to say *kaddish."*

We ought to think twice whether we honor our parents' memories by engaging in a dispute.

"Torah is good with *derech eretz*" *(Ethics of the Fathers 2:2).*

Sept. 11, 2004
Sept. 29, 2005

This is generally translated to mean that study of Torah is best when it is accompanied by an occupation whereby one can earn his livelihood. *Derech eretz* has also been translated as proper conduct, which means that scholarship should always be accompanied by courtesy.

Literally, *derech eretz* means "the way of the earth." R' Uri of Stelisk elaborated on this passage, using the literal meaning. R' Uri pointed out that the Talmud gives high praise to people who remain silent when offended. "Just think about what the earth does for us," R' Uri said. "It produces all the food we eat. It contains the various metals from which we fashion utensils for everyday living. It produces trees for shade as well as for wood to build our dwellings. Yet even though we tread upon it, it never utters a sound and it does not protest. The earth does not say, 'How dare you tread on me when I have given you so much.' That is the *derech eretz,* the way of the earth.

"A Torah scholar should have the *derech eretz,* a behavior similar to that of the earth. Even though he teaches Torah to others and many people may be the beneficiaries of his wisdom, he should remain silent when others tread upon his dignity and sensitivities. A truly devoted Torah scholar will absorb offenses without reacting to them. He should have the *derech eretz.* He should be like the earth and remain silent."

This teaching applies to everyone, not only to Torah scholars. A wise person knows that he can be the dearly beloved of G-d by refraining from reacting with hostility to anyone who slights him.

A *chassid* told the Rebbe of Rizhin that he had sinned and wished to do *teshuvah.*

"Good," the Rebbe said. "By all means, do *teshvuah.*"

"But I don't know what to do for *teshuvah,*" the *chassid* said.

"How did you know what to do to sin?" the Rebbe asked.

"I didn't," the *chassid* said. "I did what I did and then found out that it was a sin."

"Then do *teshuvah* the same way," the Rebbe said. "Stop doing what you did and you will find out that you have done *teshuvah.*"

The *chassid* thought that *teshuvah* was a ritual. The Rebbe told him the Chassidic axiom, "G-d desires the devotion of the heart." If one makes a firm commitment to never repeat the sin, *teshuvah* will then follow on its own.

From Our Heritage

NOTES

_____
_____
_____
_____
_____
_____
_____
_____
_____
_____

ELUL

אלול

Sept. 12, 2004
Sept. 30, 2005

From the Scriptures

"With their anger they killed a person"** *(Genesis 49:6).*

Chassidim point out that the Hebrew word *appam*, their anger, can also be translated as "their nose." It is possible to kill a person with a twist of the nose.

How? If someone is extolling another person's skills or good qualities, a listener may say nothing, but his grimace — the twist of his nose — essentially says, "He is not that good at all." He may not have uttered a single word, but he has communicated a powerful derogatory message. He may cause as much harm as if he had explicitly denounced that person.

Lashon hara is not limited to speech, but includes all kinds of communication. Body language is no less a form of speech than our words. Just as we must learn to control our words, we must also be careful of our gestures.

Sometimes even silence can be *lashon hara*. If we are expected to affirm a positive statement about someone and we refrain from doing so, this may be *lashon hara*. Or if a person makes a derogatory statement about someone which you know is not true and you remain silent, this too is *lashon hara*.

Of course, there may be a time when a person may be required to make a critical statement. For example, if a person is planning to enter a partnership with someone whom you know to be a crook, you have an obligation to warn that person.

Except for such circumstances, we know to be on guard against disparaging another person, whether by word, gesture, or silence.

From Our Heritage

Many of the great Torah personalities of our heritage were not only *quantitatively* greater than us, but *qualitatively* greater. It is a mistake to judge them by our standards. The Talmud says, "If the earlier generations were angels, then comparatively we are human" *(Shabbos* 112b).

R' Boruch of Mezhibozh would berate R' Levi Yitzchok of Berditchev. It appeared as though he had little regard for him as though they might have had a personal feud. One time someone said something critical of R' Levi Yitzchok, and R' Boruch reprimanded him sharply.

"But you, too, criticize R' Levi Yitzchok," the man said.

"You do not understand," R' Boruch said. "R' Levi Yitzchok is so great a *tzaddik* that the heavenly angels say to G-d 'What need do You have for a *Beis Hamikdosh* (Holy Temply) and a *Kohen Gadol*? R' Levi Yitzchok's prayers are equivalent to the services of a *Kohein Gadol*.'

"I belittle him to highlight any small imperfection he has, so that he not be accepted as a substitute for the *Beis Hamikdash*."

NOTES

_____
_____
_____
_____
_____
_____
_____
_____
_____

"If there is worry in a person's heart, let him cast it off" *(Proverbs 12:25).*

From the Scriptures

This is certainly sound advice, but often difficult to follow. How does one divest himself of worry? The Talmud suggests to relate it to another person. This is, of course, one of the values of psychotherapy. When we unburden ourselves to another person we may feel relief.

Chassidic writings give another explanation. Assume it was ordained that Reuven experience distress. When he is in distress, he speaks to his friend, Shimon, who empathizes with Reuven. But, since it was never ordained that Shimon suffer, Shimon now has unwarranted suffering. That is unjust. To eliminate this injustice, G–d removes Reuven's distress.

Sept. 13, 2004
Oct. 1, 2005

We say, "Behold, He does not slumber and does not sleep, the Guardian of Israel" *(Psalms* 121:4). Someone said, "I used to stay up at night worrying. Then I realized that G–d is going to be awake anyway. There's no point in both of us staying up."

A bit of analysis will reveal that worry is generally futile. If there is something you can do about the problem, then do it! If there is nothing you can do about it, how is worrying going to help? If anything, worry drains our energies and depresses our mood.

It renders us less capable of coping. Paradoxically, worry can actually bring about the consequences we wish to avoid.

The famous physician, Dr. Charles Mayo, said, "I have never known a man who died from overwork, but many who died from worry and doubt."

A wise person conserves his energy, finding ways to divest himself of worry.

From Our Heritage

R' Yosef Dov Soloveitchik had the reputation of being a great Torah scholar. When he became rabbi of Brisk, the townspeople were taken aback that his response to the first *she'eilah* (halachic question) posed to him was, "I don't know." When R' Yosef Dov responded similarly to the next two *she'eilos*, the townspeople held a meeting.

"Perhaps the rabbi's scholarship is of value in teaching students, but we need a rabbi who can answer our *she'eilos*," they said. They then suggested to R' Yosef Dov that he resign his position.

R' Yosef Dov smiled. "Don't worry," he said. "I can answer all your *she'eilos*. I just wanted to impress upon you that it is permissible for a rabbi to say, 'I don't know.'"

His son, R' Chaim of Brisk, recommended R' Simcha Zelig Rieger to be the *dayan* (magistrate) in Brisk. He said, "When Moshiach comes, R' Simcha Zelig will still be an outstanding *dayan*. However, his true greatness is that he can admit he does not know, and is quick to acknowledge that he erred."

Our great Torah personalities had healthy egos. They did not have to know everything, and they did not always have to be right.

NOTES

Sept. 14, 2004
Oct. 2, 2005

From the Scriptures

"If a wise man is drawn into an argument with a fool, he may be angry or he may laugh, but will have no satisfaction" *(Proverbs 29:9).*

There are no two ways about it. You cannot win an argument with a fool. Whether you are pleasant or aggressive, he will not yield. There is only one sensible thing to do: Avoid arguing with a fool.

This is also true of one who is in *denial*. He may not be a fool; he may be very intelligent. But if he has a psychological need to be oblivious of something, the most convincing logical arguments will not change his mind. Arguing with him will only make him irate.

A person had a son who was stealing from him. The father refused to believe it. He blamed the missing money on everyone except his son. In another case, a son managed to convince his father to rewrite his will to exclude other family members. No one was able to convince the father that he had been manipulated.

In such cases, one should alert the person to what is happening. "I know that you do not believe it, but I am telling you the facts. Don't close your eyes to this, because by the time you do become aware of what has happened, much harm may have been done." You do have a responsibility to try to alert a person, but after you have spoken your piece, keep quiet. Don't argue! Persistence in pressing your point will get you nowhere. In fact, the person may reinforce his position of denial.

Before you enter into an argument, stand back and size up the situation. You may find that it is impossible to win. You will spare yourself much aggravation.

From Our Heritage

When R' Velvel of Brisk was at a health resort in Switzerland, one of his visitors introduced himself as Mr. Sternovitz. R' Velvel suddenly became excited. "Did you ever reside in the town of ____?" he asked. The man responded that he did not. "Did you have a relative there, perhaps?" The man answered that his uncle had lived there, but that he was the only survivor of their large family. R' Velvel's face lit up. "I've found Sternovitz!" he cried, and asked the proprietor to set the table. "I must celebrate."

R' Velvel explained that early in World War II, his family fled for safety. Their funds ran out, and a man named Sternovitz from that town lent him money. R' Velvel promised to repay the loan when things quieted down. They had no idea that they were on the brink of the Holocaust.

"From the time I came to Israel fifteen years ago, I have been looking for a relative of Sternovitz to repay the loan. I have not had a peaceful night's sleep. Now I have someone to whom I can repay the loan."

R' Velvel had the opportunity to give the money to the rightful heir.

NOTES

_____
_____
_____
_____
_____
_____
_____
_____
_____

"The serpent said, 'If you eat of this tree, you will be like G–d, knowing good and evil'" *(Genesis 3:4).*

From the Scriptures

The Midrash tells how great Adam, the first man, was. How could he have succumbed to temptation and defy G–d's command? G–d told him that he would die if he ate of the fruit of this tree. There were other trees bearing luscious fruit. A child who is told, "This candy will make you sick. Take good candy from another table," will heed the warning. Was the great Adam less wise?

Adam was not seduced by gustatory temptation, but by the promise that, "This fruit will make you wise, as wise as G–d." Adam knew he would die. But if there was wisdom to be had, he wanted it even if it meant death. Life without wisdom is worse than death.

There is much wisdom accessible to us which carries no risk at all. Are we not foolish if we fail to avail ourselves of it?

Infinite repositories of wisdom are at our fingertips. Yet we often waste time on things that add nothing to our wisdom.

Erev
Rosh Hashanah
[Eve of
Rosh Hashanah]
Sept. 15, 2004
Oct. 3, 2005

Is it not tragic that we engage in petty disputes? They used to be of substance, such as those of Hillel and Shammai, characterized by the Talmud as being "for G–d's glory" (*Ethics of the Fathers* 5:20).

From Our Heritage

Initially, the Chassidic movement was suspected of deviation from *halachah,* arousing opposition *(misnagdim).* The *chassidim* and *misnagdim* of yore sincerely pursued "the greater glory of G–d."

My father related that when the Baal Shem Tov visited Brody, the scholars of the academy decided to drive him out of town. R' Chaim Sanzer, one of the group, remained behind, studying Torah.

That day, a woman asked R' Chaim a halachic question, and he answered that the matter was permissible. That night, R' Chaim reviewed his activities of the day, and concluded that he had erred in his answer. He had caused someone to transgress a law, and he realized this happened because he had done something else wrong. He should have joined his comrades in routing the Baal Shem.

To rectify this, R' Chaim gathered stones with which to pelt the Baal Shem Tov. The Baal Shem had already left, so R' Chaim hired a horse and wagon and followed the Baal Shem's trail.

R' Chaim reached the inn where the Baal Shem was and saw the Baal Shem reciting the morning blessings. The Baal Shem greeted him, "Rav of Brody! Your decision was correct," and proceeded to tell R' Chaim why it was so.

R' Chaim was relieved. He bid the Baal Shem Tov farewell, and as he left, he emptied his pockets of the stones he had gathered.

Here my father's eyes would well up with tears.

The Baal Shem followed R' Chaim, picking up the stones. He lifted each stone, kissed it, and put it in his pocket. "Stones picked with *kedushah* (holy intent) are sacred. They may not be on the ground."

We may have reason to differ, but disputes need not be divisive.

NOTES

Continued...

with transforming an entire community, providing a beautiful Orthodox *shul*, excellent education for the children in a Torah-oriented environment, a *mikva* and a full program of adult education courses. The Shalom Torah Academy of Englishtown-Old Bridge has also experienced phenomenal growth while assuming the role of a much needed center for both children's and adult education. Construction of a new campus for this school in Western Monmouth County was recently completed. This new state of the art facility — that is home to a Hebrew day school, afternoon Hebrew school, *shul, mikva* and community *Kiruv* center — is sure to cause Torah to flourish in this growing Jewish area.

What began as an initiative to reach out and save our children has actually come full circle with the founding and growth of the Adult Education division. Currently, close to 100 members, men and women of Shalom communities, meet on a weekly basis with scholars of the Lakewood community to study Torah and learn about *Yiddishkeit* on a one to one basis. This dynamic *Chavrusa* program has grown to include ten communities, with sessions taking place every night of the week, and many of the participants and their families becoming fully observant.

It is well known that most people drift away from the Torah and traditional Jewish values only because of ignorance. They need only be reached and they will respond. At Shalom Torah Centers, this has been proven on all levels. Whether at a *Shabbaton* weekend, an adult seminar, a weekly study session, or during the daily school curriculum, it can be seen in the profound and genuine delight that lights up the eyes of our fellow Jews as they discover the heritage that is rightfully theirs.

As Shalom Torah Centers face the future, they can point proudly to their record of achievements. They have emerged as a major force in the battle against the tide of assimilation in America. The present network of schools and programs continues to blossom; the quality of the education in both Torah related and secular subjects is uniformly excellent; parent and community response is enthusiastic. Indeed, a strong nucleus has been created; yet for every child and adult reached by Shalom Torah Centers, there are thousands more to be reached in communities across New Jersey and its neighboring states.

Yes, the future unfolds with great promise, provided, however, that there is a major investment of long hours, hard work, and new resources.

Shalom Torah Centers has various memorial and dedication opportunities available and accepts contributions in the form of wills and bequests. Arrangements for Kaddish and Yahrzeit observance can also be arranged through Shalom.

For more information please call (732) 363-5700 or 1-800-99-SHALOM